The Lotz Family

The Lotz Family

Survivors of the Battle of Franklin

J. T. Thompson and Robert Z. Carlisle II

3

The Lotz Family: Survivors of the Battle of Franklin

© 2011   J. T. Thompson and Robert Z. Carlisle II

First Edition

ISBN-13: 978-1467908252
ISBN-10: 1467908258

Front cover photograph: Courtesy of Kellye Murphy

Back cover: Photograph of Johann Albert Lotz

4

Contents

Appendix

Foreword

History is much more than dates, figures, and facts. It is a chronicle of real lives, and stories that survive the test of time.

The Lotz House tells the story of a family that experienced success, tragedy, heartbreak, and war. Johann and Margaretha Lotz suffered hardships that would destroy most families. They lost two young children in 1863 and survived one of the bloodiest battles of the American Civil War in 1864: the Battle of Franklin. The family not only endured these trials—but in fact—they thrived.

The story of Johann Lotz began in Germany in 1820. After years of hard work and training to become a master carpenter and master woodworker, Johann sailed to America in 1848. After their marriage, Johann and Margaret's journey took them to New Orleans, Cincinnati, Franklin, and eventually on a perilous and exhausting trip

9

by wagon train to California. Some of the family members survived the great San Francisco earthquake of 1906.

The Lotz family narrative includes those who became inventors, successful businessmen, artists, and professional photographers. One son—Augustus Lotz—visited Franklin on the 50th anniversary of the Battle of Franklin. Today, their daughter Matilda is considered one of the premier pioneer artists of California.

Matilda Lotz learned to draw with a stick in the dirt of Tennessee as a child, and there is little doubt that her love of animals was inspired by witnessing the moment that her pet calf was shot by a Federal soldier before the Battle of Franklin when she was only six years old. Matilda became a successful artist painting people for compensation and animals for passion. Later in life she was caught up in a second war—World War I; a war in which she lost all her precious art. The rest of her life she strived to recover them, but she was reportedly so devastated by the tragedy that she died from a broken heart in Hungary.

Houses are more than nails, bricks, and clapboards. They set, in time and place, the lives of everyday people like Matilda Lotz and her father, Johann. Their family home, the Lotz House, stands today on Columbia Avenue in Franklin, Tennessee—open to the public. Visitors are invited to hear the stories of the Battle of Franklin and view examples of Johanns' fine craftsmanship, many of Matilda's paintings, a stunning collection of antiques, and artifacts picked up off the battlefield. More importantly, Lotz House guests have the opportunity to learn about a creative and resilient family that withstood the trials and tribulations of life to leave a legacy that will stand the test of time.

Thomas Y. Cartwright

Prologue

Growing up with my father and mother there were always several givens that were never questioned. When traveling, we would always stop at every antique store, flea market and auction we would come upon. We would always visit antebellum houses throughout the South. Civil War battlefields were not to be missed and we would always live in an old home.

That is what we did. Very simple, and no ifs, ands or buts.

Being born in 1961, the Centennial year of the Civil War, it's now plain to see it was engrained in me from the moment I was conceived to have a love of history, the Civil War and all things old. Looking back I must admit I did rebel against those mandatory teachings, stops and visits. In fact, one of my earliest memories was emphatically telling both of my parents that "someday I was going to be old enough to drive, I was going to get a car and I would drive by every antique store I might be unlucky to pass." The old saying "youth is wasted on the young" certainly held true in this case. But boys will be boys and when my father ceremoniously presented me with my first ever set of

Britain's Civil War toy soldiers at the age of nine, I was hooked.

To this day, I still have those toy soldiers. I can't even begin to tell you how many times I have set them up and reenacted various Civil War battles. Growing up, my family made an annual summer pilgrimage to Middle Tennessee. We routinely visited the historic homes, plantations and mansions in the area. Belle Meade and the Hermitage were staples. But as a boy, enamored with the Civil War, The Carter House was always my favorite. I never tired of hearing the story of the bloody battle, the bravery of the soldiers, the heroics of Tod Carter and of course all of the bullet holes in the farm office and the smoke house. I devoured every book I could find on Franklin and the Civil War and while I didn't know it at the time, I was becoming a student of November 30, 1864. At the age of 15, it was announced we were moving from south Texas to Brentwood, Tennessee - just a short drive from Franklin - and I was thrilled.

Now I would be able to visit The Carter House on a much more frequent basis. You would have thought that I had died and gone to heaven, when during our first summer in Tennessee, I was actually hired as a Carter House Tour guide. I clearly remember my first day on the job and my very first tour. Anxious. You bet. But I felt up to the task. The night before I had studied all of my books, read and reread sections of Stanley Horn's "The Decisive Battle of Nashville!" I was ready. I will never forget my first tour. It was with three couples from Ohio. I walked them through The Carter House, took them to the basement, walked around the house describing the battle, the Carters and at the end of my 45-minute tour I felt confident I have given our visitors a very complete and thorough experience. I probably did! But nothing, all my work, all my study and all prep work on Franklin, the battle and The Carter House could not and did not prepare me for the one question I was asked that day. It seems our visitors had eaten breakfast before coming to The Carter House. For the first time, they had been served grits. And they loved them. The question put to me that morning on the hallowed grounds of The Carter House was "young man, can you please tell me where we can buy grit seed?" I must admit I didn't see that one coming. I blushed. I fumbled around and mumbled something about going to the co-op and buying some corn and grinding it down. Simply put, I was a crestfallen 15-year-old boy. But I learned a couple of things that day: not to take myself too seriously and no matter how much you prepare or think you know, you will inevitably be asked a question for which you don't know the answer. It is a day that I will never forget.

Acknowledgements

I would be remiss not to thank the many people who have been such a help in helping to save the Lotz House and to start the Lotz House Foundation. The list is long and I will probably forget someone, but I must thank my parents, Johnny and Sue Thompson, and my in-laws, John and Tommie Andrews. I thank my loving and adoring wife, Susan Andrews, who without her love, support and patience none of this would be possible. She is the love of my life, and without her undying love this book would never have been written. So many dear and wonderful friends have come forward to help in so many ways. Thomas Cartwright has been my rock and mentor. I am so grateful to Thomas for his guidance and wisdom. Others who have done so very much include Philip Duer, Thomas Flagel, Robert Hicks, Eric Jacobson, Doug Jones, Jim Kay, Pam Lewis, Ross Massey, Mark Shore, Margie Thessin and Rick Warwick.

Bob Carlisle, the co-author of this book, must be acknowledged for his dogged determination and patience. Never would have happened without Bob! You are a dear friend. Thank you for your guidance and your diligence. I must also thank two friends who did a great job copy editing this work, Amanda Saad and Jamie Gillum. Finally I would like very much to thank God. He has blessed me in so many ways and through him without a doubt, all things are possible. To him I give all the glory.

I ○ Discovered

Driving south down Columbia Avenue in Franklin that fateful Sunday afternoon in the late summer of 2001, I was not looking for real estate. Normally, on my daily drive I would be on the lookout for property. The perfect lot, the perfect house. But not on this day. Actually, it was the furthest thing from my mind. All I was doing was taking my daughter Shelby home to her mother's house on Battle Avenue. It was something I did every other weekend, but on this Sunday I had decided to go a different route. It was a simple diversion. That was all. As we approached the very familiar Carter House on the right, a large sign on the left side of the road caught my eye. It was a 'for sale' sign and it sat squarely in the front yard of the Lotz House. I made a mental note and promised myself I would check it out on my way back to Nashville. With Shelby delivered safe and sound a few short blocks away, I once again turned onto Columbia Avenue. This time traveling North toward Nashville.

I reached the Lotz House driveway and pulled in. I got out of the car and walked around the yard. At first glance it was the typical white, four column Greek Revival home you see so often in the South. It was a pretty plank house with brick chimneys. I loved the large magnolia and black walnut trees in the front yard. I read the state historic marker in the front of the yard, saying the home had been built by a wood worker from Germany by the name of Johann Albert Lotz. The sign continued "the Lotz Family had sought shelter with the Carters in their basement during the Battle of Franklin, November 30, 1864." It was then that I saw the bronze marker on the front of the house. I walked over to the sign to read it. "This home has been listed on the national register of historic places by the U.S. Department of Interior." My curiosity was piqued.

The next morning I called to learn more. The gentleman who answered the phone was working for the seller. He told me the home was indeed for sale, only on the market for a couple of days, and he was quick to add there was already an offer on the property. As the offer had yet to be accepted, he kindly offered to show me the house. I told him I was on my way from Nashville. I would be there in about 45 minutes.

Walking into the front hall of the Lotz House that day, I felt immediately at home. It was like I had been there before. I instinctively knew the flow of the house. And well I should. Being in old homes was certainly nothing new to me. Growing up I had always lived in old homes. In fact, by the time I left home for college I had lived in three of them. And at this point my mother was living in an old slave-made brick home down south in Lewisburg, Tennessee. But the Lotz House was different.

It was like I was seeing an old friend again. A friend that I had not seen in many years. It sounds strange but it was peaceful inside the home. Almost serene. I felt at home. I loved the wide plank yellow poplar floors. Most homes built in Tennessee during this time frame had poplar floors because termites won't eat them. The three solid wood hand-carved mantle pieces were beautiful. And the black walnut wrap around staircase was stunning. I know what most of you are thinking at this point. I know because I have lived in so many of them.

"Old houses are old houses." Most are better known as money pits. There is always something to repair, repaint or re-glue. But the Lotz House was different. For a structure 140 years old, the home was in wonderful shape. Solid, well built and sound. As I continued my tour upstairs, my mind began to race with all the possibilities. It was time to call Susan. That's my wife.

That was a fun conversation. Susan's office is located in downtown Nashville at Cummins Station. Mondays at the Public Relations and Marketing business she runs are always busy and hectic. So, you can only imagine the surprise in her voice when I said, *"I need you to come to Franklin."*

"Why?" was Susan's startled reply.

"To see the Lotz House," was my answer.

"What is the Lotz House?"

19

"It's a lovely old house, in Franklin built before the Civil War and it sits on the Franklin Battlefield. Heck it's just across the street from The Carter House."

I might as well have been speaking Greek to Susan. She was totally confused, she was quick to tell me she *"didn't know where Columbia Avenue was"* and she asked, *"what was the Battle of Franklin and who are the Carters?"*

I continued our conversation, calmly answering her questions. I explained I had stopped at the house the day before, I had gone to see it that morning, and that she needed to come check it out. All the while, fully expecting her to burst out in laughter and hang up on me. After quietly listening to my sales pitch, Susan stressed she was busy but she could be there between 3:30 and 4. I smiled, thanked her, and told her to drive safe.

II ○ Purchased

It was time. The day had arrived. We were on the way to the law office to sign the papers. And while it may sound as if it was a fairly painless decision to make, it surely was not. In the last week we had made an offer and had it accepted. We had brought Susan's parents, her sister and my mother to the house to walk through it, poke it and prod it. Susan and I had listed all the pros, all the cons on paper. We talked about it. We prayed about it. The home appraiser who walked and crawled through every nook and cranny said the home was in good shape. Of course, he said as he as wrapping things up that he had never inspected a 140 year old home. That was reassuring. But the question that lingered was, *"What are we going to do with the Lotz House?"*

Were we going to turn around and resell it? Lease it? Many of our friends asked us if we were going to move in. After a lot of thinking, research, more praying and more than one sleepless night, I boldly announced to Susan one morning, "We will open a Civil War Museum in the Lotz House." Her eyes rolled back in her head as I explained that the Sesquicentennial was rapidly approaching. And that we need to act quickly in order to get the museum established before 2011 rolled around. The first question out of her mouth was what is the "Sesquicentennial?" My answer was the "150th anniversary of the American Civil War." Again, another fun conversation.

Despite all of her concerns about my proposed museum venture, we decided to make an offer. That in itself was not a pleasant experience. Shortly after making our offer we were horrified to learn that the offer already on the table, the one I mentioned earlier, had come in significantly higher – much, much higher than ours.

We were told that the party with the higher offer had big, progressive plans for the house and property. As the house was located on a very high visible corner of Columbia Avenue in Franklin, he was going to turn the home into a Mexican food restaurant. That news didn't sit well with the owner, and so when he heard our plan to open a non profit Civil War Museum he was moved. He accepted our offer. It was there in the attorney's office on signing day that we learned even more about what might have been. Had the restaurateur gotten the home, based on the family's name spelled L-O-T-Z, he was going to name or call his Mexican restaurant "Lots of Tacos."

American marketing at its best or worst. I will let you decide.

III ∘ What we knew when we opened

Once the die was cast, the home was purchased and we knew what we were going to do with it: open a Civil War house museum. I began researching the family and the home. Spending hours on the computer, I began to acquire an incredible amount of information. I was assisted by so many wonderful local historians, but the real tipping point in my quest for information began when I found David Lotz.

David is a great, great grandson of Johann Albert Lotz. He resides today in Walnut Hills, California. David is the unofficial Lotz family genealogist and over the years had compiled a treasure trove of information and history on his family. I will never forget the first of our many conversations. It was during that initial call I learned from David how to properly pronounce his family's last name, thus the name of the house today. When we purchased the home, folks in Franklin were divided on how to say it. Some said Lots, others pronounced it Lutz and the rest

23

were convinced it was pronounced Low-tz. When David answered the phone I introduced myself, told him who I was and why it I was calling and I asked him as he was a direct descendent of the builder, "How do you pronounce your last name?"

I could hear him smile on the other end of the line and he confidently replied, my last name is pronounced "Low-tz" spelled "L-O-T-Z.' Over the course of the next several months we exchanged phone calls and emails, and the story of this incredible American family with its roots in Germany began to take shape.

Today when you talk about the Lotz House, you must start with the man who built it. Johann Albert Lotz was born in Saxony, Germany in 1820. His mother died shortly after his birth. No doubt not having his mother affected him growing up. And as young boy, Johann's father insisted it was time for him to go to work. And go to work he did, in the European Guild System.

Initially he would serve as a lowly apprentice, after seven years was promoted to the position of Journeymen, which meant he could actually be paid for the work he was doing. And finally after almost 20 years of very hard work, study and extensive travel throughout Germany and Switzerland, Johann earned the prestigious European title of master woodworker, master carpenter. In researching this story, I wanted to know more about the guild process and what steps were actually required to achieve the designation of master woodworker. It's an arduous path, one that involves studying architecture, engineering and mathematics, but also mastering the skills of using your hands to build, make and shape things out of wood. Very specific proficiency tests had to be taken and passed for one to advance. I learned the last test a journeyman was required to take to achieve the title of master woodworker was to design and build a staircase. This was a truly a monumental task, as at that time no two homes, no two floors of a house would ever be the same. To make the staircase fit into a home was truly an extraordinary engineering feat. Today, when you look at the incredible staircase Johann built in his own home in Franklin, it's crystal clear he was a very capable student who learned his lessons very, very well.

After earning his woodworking degree, Johann and wife Margaretha decided to come to the States to capitalize on his 20 year college education. His first American soil was New Orleans in 1849. He would no doubt be influenced by the incredible woodworking and furniture building that was being done there at that time. In fact, some of the finest furniture made in America during that time frame was handcrafted in New Orleans. From there, research indicates that Margaretha and Johann traveled to the Cincinnati, Ohio area and may have visited his father and an older brother who had immigrated to America before Albert. After a two year stay there, Johann and Margaretha headed south and moved to Tennessee, arriving in Franklin in 1854. But why the sleepy, small and rural town of Franklin? Why not the bustling city of Nashville? At first glance, Nashville might appear to be a much better choice, significantly larger and with a much bigger customer base for a German master woodworker.

But unlike Nashville, Franklin did give Albert an immediate and cheaper supply of the lumber needed for his craft. It provided him an almost limitless supply of quality hard woods: poplar, chestnut and black walnut. Undoubtedly, his cost would be decidedly cheaper in Franklin as opposed to Nashville. And there was another important consideration. By setting up shop in Franklin, he would have very little competition.

A year later, Lotz purchased the property and began to build his first home, today located at 1111 Columbia Avenue. At the time, on the outskirts of Franklin, it was in the country and very quiet, serene and very, very different when compared to all the traffic that drives by the house today. Lotz purchased five acres from Fountain Branch Carter whose lovely brick home sat just across the street. It seems odd to us today that Carter would end up selling the narrow stretch of land so very close to his home and 300 acre farm. But it made perfect sense for Carter. A successful farmer and business man, Carter was what today we call an entrepreneur. Besides his vast productive farmland, he had his cotton gin and it is well known that Carter was frequently buying and selling property. The tract that Lotz purchased from Carter was very long and narrow and basically ran the width of the property line, which sits on Columbia Pike today. It ran east almost to Lewisburg Pike. As it turns out, the property sits on a small hill, called Carter Hill at the time. You see from Carter's perspective the small piece of land was too rocky for him to farm. On the edge of his property it was wasted ground. Therefore, Carter was willing to sell the unproductive real estate to Lotz and pocket the extra cash.

While Lotz knew his small parcel of land would never produce lush and profitable farm crops, he did know for the home he planned to build it would be the perfect place for his first American show house. He would build his home, and then invite potential customers to his house. He would point out all of the woodworking and intricate designs at his home and what he had done for he and his family, and then he would say, "What would you like for me to do for you and your family?" No doubt, Lotz was a wonderful woodworker, master builder and master carpenter. In our world today we would call him a great salesman, marketer and public relations person as well!

It took Lotz three years to build the home. He did this without slaves and slave labor. He built it by himself. One must remember Lotz is German. He had grown up in Europe and slaves and slavery were not ingrained in his upbringing. Certainly, he and his family were used to seeing slaves. Carter, just across the street, had several according the 1860 Franklin census. But when it came to Lotz and his home, Lotz did not rely on anyone else to build it. He used his own two hands.

When you reflect upon what that means today, it's truly a marvel. To think he would build, cut and saw every piece of wood, and hammer every nail by himself, it is mind boggling given our use of power tools today. But remember, up until this point he had spent virtually his entire adult life learning how to master wood. If anything, everything he had previously undertaken in life was in done in preparation for what he was about to do in Franklin. One of the most touching aspects of this story is what Lotz built first on his newly acquired property. There's no doubt he wanted all the residents of Franklin to know his intentions. Prior to starting on the foundation of his home, he surrounded the property, all five acres, with a wonderful three plank wooden fence. It's this very same fence that the Federal army would find very beneficial on the morning of November 30, 1864.

During the next several months anyone and everyone traveling up and down Columbia Pike saw the Lotz Home taking root and beginning to take shape. What a site it must have been. When finished, his home would be exactly what Lotz had intended it to be: a show house, a resume, a complete catalogue, a three dimensional example of the work he was capable of producing, making and carving out of wood. Above the portico was a large intricate acanthus leaf scroll with vines, leaves and large c-scrolls. For passersby the acorn finials on the eaves that run the entire roof line would have been hard to miss as would the large flowers on the top of each of four large square columns on the front of the house.

It must have been interesting to look above each of the windows and see the carving above each one and see that the first floor carving was totally and uniquely different from the carving on the second floor. From Lotz's perspective it was a wonderful way to literally showcase his woodworking. He could clearly tell his potential customers to look at the carving over the first floor windows and compare it to the carving over the second floor windows. It was a way for them to personally choose which design they wanted. In effect Lotz was offering a very early example of great customer service in the mid 19^(th) century, not to mention incredible woodworking.

Once you step into the home today you can still see Lotz's mastery of wood. The crown moldings, the millwork throughout the house as well as the cornices above each of the windows and doors are all examples of his handiwork. Three original fireplace mantles also remain in the home. Each of the mantles were carved out of a different kind of wood, black walnut, cherry and chestnut. Each also has a different level of design or carving on it, again showing his clients that he brought his versatility to his home. But it's the handrail on the stair case that perhaps is the most awe inspiring example of Lotz woodworking.

Crafted entirely of black walnut, it twists and turns and bends all the way to the second floor. Amazing! It's plain to see that Johann Albert Lotz loved working with wood. He also loved music and made wonderful musical instruments, including guitars, banjos, fiddles as well as grand pianos. In fact, the newel post of the staircase in his home is one of the large heavy legs from one of his pianos that Lotz inverted and used to stabilize his black walnut staircase. When you see the symmetry of his work today, it's safe to say that indeed Lotz was a superlative woodworker, a sculptor and to a great extent a very accomplished artist.

His accomplishments in wood and his glorious show house garnered him plenty of work. He carved furniture and fireplace mantles for the Williamson County Court

House when it opened in Franklin in 1858. Pre-war, he did extensive woodworking for both Saint Cecilia and Saint Bernard in Nashville. And post war, he did extensive woodworking at the Athenaeum in Columbia. Despite leaving the small town of Franklin, it's evident he was traveling the mid-state working his wares.

We have recently learned he may have even traveled into Southern Kentucky and worked on some homes in Russellville, Kentucky. This news warrants more research on my part and we will include what we find in our next book.

After the 1860 census was taken in Franklin, twins, a boy and girl, were born to the Lotz Family. Their names were Julian and Julius. And in the spring of 1863, those toddlers were two and a half years old. Both drank from a water well or a water source that had been poisoned, contaminated by the Federal Army and both of those babies tragically died. It's safe to say both Lotz and his wife had issues dealings with the Federal army 18 months before the Battle of Franklin erupted in their front yard.

Having researched this family for the last 10 years, I personally have a problem accepting this incredibly sad story. If the source was a water well, why was the rest of the family not affected? Despite the atrocities that took place in war time, on both sides, it wasn't common practice for soldiers, both North and South, to poison wells. Therefore, I would like to put forth another theory to explain this Lotz twin's tragedy.

In the spring of 1863, Franklin was occupied by the Federal Army. Martial law had been declared. Citizens were required to sign an oath of allegiance, and they had to obtain a pass if they wished to travel outside of town. The Federal army was hard at work constructing the earthen works of Fort Granger. It was also at this time that Federal troops began to dig the entrenched line approximately 200 yards to the south of the Lotz House. It's the very same trench line that played such a critical role during the Battle of Franklin on November 30, 1864. It's because the trench line had already been started in 1863 that the Federal Army was able to so quickly strengthen it, making it much deeper and stronger before the Battle of Franklin started.

Thus my theory. It's late March, early April of 1863 and the Lotz's twins were like all small children. They were running and playing outside on the land that surrounds their home. A strong spring storm moved across Williamson County and quickly dumped rain, filling the trench with two or three feet of water. The twins accidently fell headfirst into the trench and quickly drowned. I stress this is a theory, but certainly a plausible one. Nonetheless, according to each and every Lotz letter, diary and family story, the twins died after drinking from a water well or water source that had been poisoned or contaminated by the Federal army. The long and short of it; we will probably never know the whole story. But the fact remains, no matter if it was a tragic accident or an intential act, Johann and his Margaretha went to their graves believing the Federal army, Northern soldiers, were responsible for the deaths of Julian and Julius.

There were three small children in the home on the day of the battle. The oldest son Paul was nine years old. The little girl of the family was named Matilda. Her family called her Tillie for short, a sweet nickname. Born in the house in 1858, the year the house was completed, Matilda celebrated her sixth birthday in the house the day before the Battle of Franklin. The baby of the family was named Augustus. He was only two years old. And we have now learned another family member was living with the Lotz at this point. Her name was Amelia, 13 or 14 years of age. She was a Margaretha's daughter from an earlier marriage.

What's important to remember is that the Lotz family, the Carters across the street, the McGavocks a mile away at Carnton Plantation and about 750 people in downtown Franklin all went to sleep on Tuesday night, November 29, 1864, not having a clue what was headed their way in less than 12 hours time.

The town was awakened early on the morning of November 30. Tough to imagine this today that literally 20,000-22,000 Federal troops and horses, wagons and cannons were marching down Columbia Pike headed north to Nashville. They were under orders to get to Nashville quickly, but as soon as this huge army, complete with a supply wagon train stretching eight miles down the highway gets just north of town, they run into a problem. The problem was the Harpeth River. It had been a very wet fall in Middle Tennessee and the water in the Harpeth was too high for the army to cross over. The county bridge was down and the pontoon boats that had been ordered from Nashville to Franklin had yet to arrive.

Simply put, the Federal army was stuck. Trapped. In today's world we would describe it as traffic gridlock on the interstate. Hundreds of supply wagons and mule teams were backed up bumper to bumper in downtown Franklin. Total chaos. The Federal commander, John McAlister Schofield had some engineers traveling with his army. He ordered them to quickly start repairing the bridge and he would send the bulk of the army back south of town and they would begin to strengthen the entrenched line.

At the Lotz House, between 10:15 and 10:45 that morning, the Federal army knocked on Lotz's front door. They told Lotz they intended to do some yard work for him that day. I say that facetiously. In all seriousness, the northern soldiers went out behind his home and tore down his barn, stable, out house, smokehouse and detached kitchen. They leveled his all important woodworking shop. They removed every splinter of wood. The Federal army cut down every tree on his property. Remember that wonderful plank fence that Lotz had first built on his newly purchased property? The Federals mowed the fence down and used all of the wood, lumber and building materials to fortify and strengthen the breast works on the entrenched line.

Then it was time to eat. The Federal soldiers went behind Lotz's home and began to slaughter cows, hogs, sheep and chickens. I like to remind our guests when they visit us today that the Lotz House is a solid wood plank, clapboard house. When you are inside you can hear the traffic driving up and down Columbia Avenue. When the wind blows, when the bird sing, when the thunder rolls, you can easily hear it. There's no doubt, the day of the battle, the Lotz's family huddled in their home and could easily hear the commotion that surrounded their home. When the Federal army cut the Lotz Family cow and it screamed and moaned, the family could hear it. I encourage everyone to take a step back and put themselves in the place of Mr. and Mrs. Lotz. Just 18 months earlier at the hands of the Federal Army, the same army doing the damage to their property that day, they had buried two babies. Today, it is safe to say at that time, the Lotz were filled with nothing but sheer, utter terror.

Around 2 p.m. on November 30, the Confederate army began to arrive two miles south of the Lotz home at Winsted Hill. Confederate Commander John Bell Hood ordered a direct frontal assault against the heavily entrenched and fortified Federal army. The southern Battle line stretched for three miles facing north into Franklin. Over the course of that afternoon, Johann Albert Lotz, from his front yard, looked south across those two miles of open fields. He saw the tidal wave of brown and gray uniforms forming, and he recognized that he and his family were in very serious trouble. After all, they lived in a solid wooden plank house. Later that afternoon, Lotz picked up his baby in one arm and his tool box in the other. Margaretha grabbed Matilda's hand and Paul and Amelia followed close behind. The family dashed out the front door of their home, they ran south through all of the Federal soldiers and they went 110 steps across the street to the front door of the Carter House where they were welcomed with open arms.

The Carter House is made of brick with a large brick basement and Lotz understood if there was a chance to survive the storm that was headed their way, their odds were much better in the brick Carter House as opposed to the wooden planked Lotz House.

In terms of the battle, I will not attempt to describe it. Too many other scholarly and learned historians have already written so much and done it so much better than I ever could. I am so grateful to them for their research and hard work because it's their scholarly efforts that continue to keep the Battle of Franklin alive today.

But I will say this: when all was said and done on the evening of November 30, you could walk out the front doors of the Lotz House, spin in any direction you want to look, and you would have witnessed approximately 10,000 casualties. Today when you see all the cars, trucks and motorcycles going up and down the road it is hard to imagine. That's why I like to give folks this analogy to help them put the unspeakable carnage into perspective: what happened in Franklin is the equivalent to three days of September 11, 2001 back to back to back.

The little one-horse town of Franklin witnessed that same death and destruction in five short hours. Bodies of soldiers were described as five and six feet deep and stacked like cord wood. I think the best, if not the worst description, is that bodies of dead soldiers both North and South stood like scarecrows. They could not fall for the dead at their feet. In the Lotz House yard, 17 horses were dead. It's a cliché that is often overused, but it proves to be true in this case: what happened to the small country town of Franklin, the few families that called it their home and most importantly, to those families and their children, November 30, 1864 was hell on earth.

IV ○ Post-Battle

Lotz and his family survived in the brick basement across the street for 19 long, arduous hours. I don't have the words or the understanding to begin to express or relate what they must have heard, saw, thought, or smelled while the battle raged all around them. The words frightening or unspeakable seem so very inappropriate - almost shallow. But I do know this. The following morning, on their short walk home from the front door of The Carter House to The Lotz House, just 110 steps, none of the Lotz family was able to take a step without stepping on the body of dead American soldier.

When Lotz got home he was relieved to know that he made the right decision to seek refugee across the street.

He walked into what remained of his show house and turned into the first room on the left. There he saw where a six pound solid shot Confederate cannon ball blasted through the roof, crashed through the second floor and landed on the floor. Today, when you walk into the room, you can still see the large, burned depression where that ball landed.

Visitors to the home today will notice that there are wonderful large windows on every side of the home, both upstairs and downstairs, except for the south wall. Pre-battle there were windows on the south side of the home as well, but after the battle the wall was heavily damaged and full of bullet holes. Due to the war torn broken economy, if you could find glass windows, it was difficult paying for them. Therefore, Lotz was forced to repair the wall without replacing the windows.

Lotz wanted a reminder of that tragic day, and today we have a reminder as well. After the battle he cut out a section of the damaged south wall. In it you can clearly see two large holes that pierced the entire width of the 4 inch thick wall. One hole is caused by canister, a shotgun blast from a cannon. The second, smaller hole was caused by a bullet or Minnie ball. It is a grim and graphic reminder of that bloody November day.

Upstairs in the home today, more battle damage is clearly evident. During the battle, the staircase, much of the hallway, the banister, basically the center of his entire home came crashing down. We know that by looking at the way the master woodworker repaired his war scarred show house. As his woodworking shop was destroyed and the wood it once contained was now shot to bits in the breast works during the battle, Lotz was forced to go out and search for wood in the middle of winter to repair his home. The only wood he could find quickly and in short order was red pine or sugar pine, also known as heart of pine. The pine is a very pretty wood. It's also very susceptible to termite damage. A master woodworker would never use pine to repair his home unless he was forced to.

Battle damage to the home is also quite evident by the two upstairs fireplaces. Today, both of them have been bricked in. Before the battle, the upstairs fireplaces shared a flue with both the downstairs fireplaces. After the battle, the south wall of the home and the upstairs were so damaged that Lotz was forced to come back home and brick in the upstairs fireplaces, relying on the efficient coal burning fireplaces on the first level to heat the upstairs. Today, when you see consider the kind of decisions he had to make, you begin to grasp the gravity of the situation. The decision to block up the flues was based on one thing: survival. The weather in December 1864, the month following the battle, didn't help Lotz much. That December was a brutally cold month with terrible ice and snow. In fact, the winter of 1864-1865 was one of the coldest in Middle Tennessee history.

There's one more battle scar in the home I must tell you about. Remember that cannonball that crashed through the home landing on the first floor and leaving the large burn mark and indention? In the room directly above the indention, you can see the patch in the floor that Lotz was forced to repair. He had none of the precious termite resistance wood to use in the patch so he had to use

39

chestnut. Upon closer inspection you can see something else. The planks are not lined up. He left large gaps in the repair work and hammered in the nails so hard he actually dented the wood. Certainly not the kind of repair work one would expect from a master woodworker twenty years in the making.

You see, when he was making these repairs, it was not about being pretty nor being perfect. It was about hastily getting it done and repairing the home quickly. Survival! And when you look at these elementary repairs, you do begin to see Lotz's mental state at this point. There's fear, anxiety, frustration and the way he was pounding those nails you can see he was also very, very angry. Why wouldn't he be?

Today when you visit the Lotz House, you see a large red flag flying from the second story balcony on the outside of the house. I tell our visitors that red flag was a 19th century version of instant messaging. Meaning, as soon as the battle ended any and every building left standing, be it the church, the Masonic lodge, a tool shed or a barn, became immediately used as a hospital.

All of the sites flew a red flag or a red piece of material. It let everyone know as they passed by that it was a hospital site. Today, blood stains remain on every floor of the home. They are especially heavy in corners, along walls and under windows. Surgeons desperately needed the light from those windows, plus an open window provided them a quick, convenient way to discard severed limbs. At the time of the battle, the floors of the home were covered with carpet or area rugs. Today, you can see where the blood soaked through the carpet, leaving elongated stains. In the front keeping room in particular you can see where two, three or more soldiers were leaning up against the wall, the blood soaking through the carpet. There was so much blood in fact that it actually caused the wooden floors to warp. When you see blood stains of that magnitude, it's a sobering thought to know the home housed a great deal of dead and dying American soldiers immediately following the battle.

After returning to the house the following morning, Lotz and his family were forced to set up residence in what was basically a root or vegetable cellar on the north side of the house. Lotz, as previously noted, began to repair his home as quick and as best as he could. Given the broken Southern economy post war , there was indeed very little money to hire or commission a master carpenter to do anything, let alone make or sell any musical instruments. Life had to be very difficult for the Lotz Family in terms of just providing for the children, but if we've learned anything at this point about Johann Albert Lotz, he was not a quitter. He was able to find enough work to sustain his family.

In June of 1869, he decided he would carve another grand piano. This musical instrument was much different than the ones he had previously made. This piano was special to Lotz as it represented that the terrible Civil War was over and our divided country was now united. On the top of this grand piano he carved a huge American eagle with outstretched wings. On one side he carved the

41

Federal or US flag. On the other side he carved the Confederate battle flag.

For a reason we do not know, he carved the eagle's claws, or its talons, clutching, grabbing, digging into the Confederate flag. We don't know what his intensions or motivations were for carving the piano in that way. It could have been an expression of his creativity, or it could have been a decision he made prompted by the graining of the wood he was using. Some suggest it could have been the show of Northern dominance of the South. We just don't know.

One thing we do know is that Pulaski, Tennessee, Giles County is approximately one hour south of Franklin. It's the community that is the birthplace of the Ku Klux Klan. The KKK was very active in Middle Tennessee in the summer of 1869. In fact, Federal troops were garrisoned in Franklin well into 1868 because of what the Klan was doing or threatening to do in Middle Tennessee. The Klan heard about Lotz's piano and came to the home to check it out. When they saw it, they were incredulous - total outraged with Lotz, because they felt he had shown total disrespect to the Confederate flag by having the eagle desecrate the Confederate flag.

A war of words erupted between Lotz and the Klan. That argument worsened, festered, intensified over the next several weeks, and it reached a point that Lotz learned the Klan had plans for him. They were going to make an example out him to the people of Franklin and at the same time, teach the German immigrant a lesson. They intended to march him out into his very own front yard and tar and feather him, a terrible, painful and humiliating way to die.

Upon learning that news, Lotz wasted little time and took action of his own. Within days he sold his home, the piano inside the house, everything he owned for pennies on the dollar or gave it away. He purchased a covered wagon. It's in that wagon he took his family 2,300 miles safely across Indian territory to San Jose, California. The Klan scared the dickens out of Lotz and he moved his family as far from Franklin, Tennessee as possible.

At the time I wrote this book, the house is 153 years old. During that timeframe it has been used by many people for many different things. It has been a private residence, attorney's office, submarine sandwich shop, bakery, flower shop, apartment house, florist and used as haunted house for several years during Halloween.

Lotz got to California and did well for himself. He made pianos and he opened a prosperous carriage making business utilizing his woodworking skills. Paul, the oldest son, worked within the family business for a while and then moved to San Francisco to make a name for himself. He went work for Elite Photography, a state-of-the-art photography company. He later purchased Elite Photography and business thrived. Paul survived, but his business did not due to the San Francisco earthquake and subsequent fire. He moved to New York City. We do not know why. He died there several years later from a heart attack.

The youngest child, Augustus, two at the time of the battle, has a tremendous life story. He was the only immediately family member to ever return to Franklin for a visit. He actually traveled back to Tennessee on the 50th anniversary of the battle. Of course, he had no memories of the terrible battle and the difficult times afterward. As an adult, Augustus was known as a tinker - an inventor - and always was a wonderful piano player, no doubt learning on the fine instruments his father made.

Augustus held many U.S. patents. He made a small fortune in the early canning business in Monterey, California. He sold his business to a partner and took his family, a wife and three daughters, to Philadelphia where it is believed he went to work for a man named Mr. Hoover and the two were credited with inventing the vacuum sweeper.

But it's Matilda who, in both life and death, is the rock star of the family. And it's Matilda that clearly paints a picture of how the Battle of Franklin will affect and ultimately influenced the lives of the civilians of the town.

You'll recall Matilda was born in the Lotz House in 1858. As a little girl she went out back behind her parents' home and meticulously began to draw the family farm animals in the dirt with a stick.

Once the family got to California post war, Matilda continued with her art. With the help of a very special lady, Phoebe Hurst, mother of William Randolph Hurst, Matilda applied to and was accepted into the French Academy. At the time, that was the finest art school in the world. Matilda excelled in Paris. In fact, she was the first woman to win two gold medals at the Paris Salon. After she finished her studies, she returned to California to see her mom and dad.

While back, she found time to paint a portrait of Mr. Hurst as well as Governor Leland Stanford, founder of Stanford University. At the age of 25, almost 26, she looked her parents in the eye and said she was going to return to Europe and paint. Unheard of! Scandalous! No chaperone? Matilda, undeterred, returned to Europe. Befriended by the Duke of Portland, she stayed long enough at his summer estate outside of London to paint his prize racing horses. She traveled across the continent. This young woman was so fearless, so unafraid, as she boarded a small boat by herself and sailed all the way down the Nile River to Egypt where she spent the next ten years of her life painting camels, the pyramids, and the streets of Cairo.

Today, Matilda is recognized as one of California's premier female pioneer artists. Her art is hard to come by, highly prized and collected on our west coast as well as all of Europe where she spent most of her adult life. I'd like to remind you at this point, it was on the day after Matilda's 6th birthday that she saw, touched, smelled, felt, tasted, experienced and lived through The Battle of Franklin in her own yard. In and around her home it would be that day, November 30, 1864, that empowered and emboldened her to lead this life.

Matilda made her money in Europe. She had studios in both London and Paris. It was there she painted wealthy people, special people and members of various royal families, but Matilda's passion and escape was always a return to her roots to paint very simple and basic farm animals. On the morning of the battle, Matilda, that little six year old girl, witnessed her pet calf shot in the head. It was that very sad moment in her life that she never forgot.

Late in life, Matilda was asked to travel to Hungary, where she met and painted a portrait of Emperor Joseph, the Hungarian King. Upon meeting her he was so impressed with Matilda he saw to it that she had a studio built in Budapest. Then, at the age of 55, this independent, strong woman determined it was time for her to settle down. She was introduced to and fell in love with an Austrian Count, who also was an artist. The couple was happily married for ten years until her death in 1923 at 65 years of age. Matilda's life story was an incredible and fantastic story, and one that took a very interesting twist and turn on November 30, 1864.

It was with this wonderful family story that we were set to open the Lotz House Civil War house museum.

V ∘ Meeting Bob Carlisle

The Lotz House opened on Friday, October 29, 2008, with a ribbon cutting and private party for friends and supporters. Opening the home had been a dream for so many years and we received support from so many in Franklin as we began this venture. We were about three weeks in when a very kind gentleman named Bob Carlisle and his daughter Cathy McMullen, who works for the National Park Service, walked into the home. I gave them a tour and the rest, as they say, is history.

Bob sent me an email and politely told me he and Cathy had enjoyed their tour very much. In fact, Bob told me his daughter said it was one of the best tours she had ever taken. He proceeded to tell me that he was an amateur genealogist and was so moved by the Lotz family's story that he would like to volunteer to research the family.

It was so nice to hear that they had enjoyed their tour and I promised myself I would call him and move forward. But life happens, and I was busy trying to get the Lotz House off the ground, so I didn't respond to Bob's kind note. Thank goodness Bob was not put off.

About 10 days later he called me and again thanked me for a wonderful tour and graciously offered to research the family. We made an appointment for the next day. I handed him all of my research and he said he would get to work. Bob was quick to say he would try his best, but that he couldn't promise anything. I was just so thrilled someone was interested in the family. I shook his hand, said thank you and walked him to the door.

It was only a couple of days later that Bob sent an email, reporting that he had found information about the Lotz in Germany. This continued almost every five or six days. Bob would call, email, stop by the house and show me his latest find. And now, more than two years later, Bob continues his work and routinely finds new information on the Lotz and their place in history. What follows is Bob's intensive, laborious research on the family, the house and their story. We know so much more about the Lotz that without Bob's diligence might have been lost to history. Bob did all this selflessly. He spent his own time, energy and money to discover what you are about to read. Thank you Bob for all you have done, all you continue to do, and most of all, for being a very dear friend to the Lotz family, their story, and to me. It's my pleasure to introduce you to Robert Z. Carlisle II.

Johann Albert Lotz (circa 1900) at about 70 years of age.

August Lotz (circa 1865) at about 4 years of age.

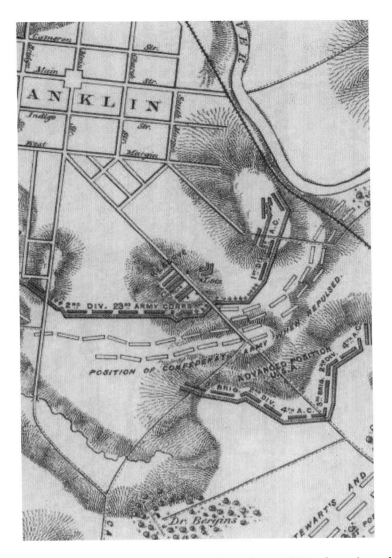

U. S. Army Engineer Map published in 1874 showing the Lotz House in the center of the map, just inside the Federal lines. (Courtesy of the Library of Congress)

"*Sheep at Rest*" by Matilda Lotz circa 1880
On display at the Lotz House.

Johann Albert Lotz. Photograph taken by Paul Lotz.

Albert and Margareta Lotz's headstone at Oakhill Cemetery in San Jose, California.

Matilda Lotz as a young woman in California.

Margareta Lotz in 1878, San Jose, California at 48 years old.

The Artist – Matilda Lotz.

Ornate hand-carved table by master craftsman—Johann Albert Lotz.

Nora King and Steve Hays with Albert's hand-carved table.

"*The Donkey*" by Matilda Lotz circa 1880
On display at the Lotz house.

"*The Herd*" by Matilda Lotz circa 1885-86
On display at the Lotz House.

"*The Wolf*" by Matilda Lotz circa 1870
On display at the Lotz House.

The "Friends of the Painter"—a field, two dogs and an artist's knapsack—is signed "Matilda Lotz, 1884," and she hails from Tennessee. What enormous progress she has made, too, since I first knew her on her arrival in Paris in 1879. We may have seen each other before that for all I know, for she once told me that when she was a little child she was an eye witness to one of the great battles of the civil war in which I took a part. Her parents lived out on what was known as the Granny White turnpike just beyond Nashville, and when Gen. George H. Thomas was manœuvering us against Gen. Hood's brave army we tramped and fought over pretty much all the roads and farms of that part of Middle Tennessee. One day little Matilda Lotz sat on a rail fence and saw men and horses shot down all around her and she never flinched or cried; but when a stray bullet killed a pet calf and her mama told her 'twas the Yankees that did it, she burst into tears and said that she hated us. She is just as brave and good to-day as she was them; chockful of talent which finds vent in painting animals, and, mark my prediction, some of us not yet out of our forties will live to see her name take rank with that of Rosa Bonheur's.

An article from the New Orleans newspaper *Times Picayune* dated May 18, 1884.

"The Lotz House" by Frederick Detcher

VI ○ Lotz Family History

Johann Albert Lotz Family

An Immigrant Footprint That Made a Difference.

With the opening of the Lotz House Museum in 2008, an opportunity was created for visitors from around the world to hear the exciting story of an American immigrant family who was caught in the middle of one of the bloodiest days of the Civil War. On the afternoon of November 30, 1864, Albert Lotz gathered his family and fled across the street to the basement of the

Carter home, seeking shelter from the advancing Confederate troops. Memories of the carnage the children witnessed the next morning and experiencing the resilience of their parents would influence these children for the rest of their lives. Each of the Lotz children would become well known for the contribution they would make to America's rapid progressive changes at the turn of a new century.

Albert Lotz arrives in America

Johann Albert Lotz was born in Meiningen, Saxony, Germany on August 18, 1820. Records from the Pfarramt Evangelical Lutheran Church indicate Albert was born on August 19, but he always used the 18th. His parents were Ludwig Heinrich Lotz and Sophie Friederike Christine Eleonore Hofling. Sophie died on September 15, 1820, six weeks after Albert was born. Church records indicate that Albert's father immigrated to the United States in 1833. His brother Johann Friedrich Lotz also went to America. By 1840, Albert applied for a Professional Work Record (Wanderbook), which would record all his travels through the next few years as he became a master of his cabinet making trade. This book was his passport and remained with him for the rest of his life. It stated that he had blond hair, a wide forehead, grey blue eyes, a round chin and no special marks. He would never return to his home town of Meiningen.

He worked in Esslingen, Germany from 1840 to 1843, Mainz in 1843, Kehl and Konstanz in 1844. Then, by May of 1844, he was in Zurich, Switzerland. He was in Bern by May of 1845 and Neuchatel, Switzerland in July of 1847. Albert entered France on July 24, 1847. Then on September 16, 1848, he arrived in the port city of La Havre on the English Channel. All this time he honed his skills as a master carpenter preparing himself for what would become a life full of creative construction opportunities. Traveling as a single man with no family, Albert arrived in the port of New Orleans, Louisiana, November 27, 1848 on the French ship, Anna. The ship passenger list states that Albert was 28 years old.

Albert met Margareta Grass (Grasz) and her two children, Joseph and Amelia, probably about 1850. Albert was listed in the 1850 census on August 7 in New Orleans, living by himself. Margareta (Margaret) was married while in Germany. Her home was in Bavaria but both of her children were born in Saxony. Great-grandson, David Lotz of California states, "It is believed she was a young divorcee with two small children, Joseph and Amelia. Her married name is not known with any degree of certainty, but is believed to have been either Fields or Shields." Family history states that Margareta left Germany with her children, fleeing an abusive marriage. No record has been found of Albert and Margaret's marriage. It is assumed they were married before leaving Louisiana. Margareta (Margaret) was born on February 14, 1820 in Bavaria, Germany.

David Lotz has written that Albert and his new family left New Orleans in the early 1850s for Covington, KY. They stayed there for a short time and moved to Warren Co. Ohio. In about 1854, the family moved south to Nashville, TN. This is all verified from an article which was written on Margaret's oldest son, Joseph A. Lotz, in the *History of San Clara County, CA,* 1881. By 1855, the family had purchased property in Franklin, Williamson County, TN. On May 24, 1855, Albert filed for his intention for naturalization and citizenship. He received his citizenship on July 18, 1859. Because of the father's naturalization, his wife and children were then considered citizens.

On August 29, 1855, Albert Lotz bought Lot 114 on Bridge St. between 3rd and 4th Streets in Franklin for $600. Albert sold this home on December 25, 1865 for $900. During the time the family lived in downtown Franklin he operated his piano manufacturing and repair business out of his home. This is substantiated in an advertisement that ran in the *Franklin Review,* dated July 20, 1855. The same advertisement ran on January 25, 1856, stating his residence was on Bridge Street.

Albert builds home in Franklin

On March 5, 1858 Albert bought five acres of land south of downtown Franklin for $1,000 from

Fountain Branch Carter. The property was located just north of the Carter home and on the east side of Columbia Pike. It is on this property that Albert Lotz, master carpenter built his beautiful antebellum, two-story home. It is unclear the date construction began or when the family moved from the downtown location to their new home. We do know Albert and Margaret's second child Matilda was born in their new home in November 1858. The family continued to live in this home until they moved to California near the end of 1869 or the beginning of 1870. The property was sold on January 22, 1870 for $3,000. The deed states, "The piano and melodian now in the house is included in the purchase."

Albert and Margaret's first child, Paul, was born February 23, 1855 in Nashville, TN. Matilda came on November 29, 1858. Family history states that twins, Julie and Julius, were born in about 1860. Both children died at about age four after drinking contaminated water from a home pond. One story says that the Yankees had poisoned the pond so the Confederate soldiers could not use it. No record has been found of the twin's birth, death or a cemetery plot. The youngest child, Augustus, was born on August 15, 1861.

The Lotz and Carter homes were at the epicenter of the Battle of Franklin, which was a pivotal battle in the Civil War on November 30, 1864. By the afternoon of the 30th it was clear to Albert Lotz that his wood framed home would not be safe for his family. Mr. Carter invited Albert to bring his family to safety in the basement of his home, which was built with brick. There were four Lotz children present during the Battle: Amelia - age 17, Paul - age 9, Matilda – age 6, and Augustus – age 3. Joseph, now 23 had left home and was probably living in Nashville or Louisville, KY.

Following the Battle, Albert found his home had sustained major damage from cannon and gun fire. As with many homes in the area, the Lotz House was used as a hospital following the Battle. Before winter arrived, and during the next few months, Albert worked tirelessly to repair the damage and restore their home to its original beauty. Today there are no windows on the south side of the home. This apparently is due to the heavy damage that was sustained during the battle and Albert's need to ready the house for winter. Even today one can see the burn marks of cannon balls on the floors of the Lotz home. The family continued to live in Franklin for the next five years.

The following letter dated, March 21, 1865, was submitted by Albert Lotz to the United States government in hopes of compensation for his family's property loss during the Battle of Franklin. Note the listing of "one cow slaughtered," which was undoubtedly daughter Matilda's pet calf and the reference by Lt. Col. Matzdorff to Albert's loyalty to the Union.

Major Gen'l. L. H. Rosseau
Comd'g District of Tennessee

General:

I beg leave to submit to you the following statement of losses and property sustained by me through the U.S.

Troops at the time of the Battle of Franklin, Nov. 30, 1864, with a view to receive just compensation therefore:

4000 feet of plank fences with posts used in erection of breastworks $750.00

One Stable torn down for same purpose
$250.00

One Chicken House torn down for same purpose
$100.00

Lumber for Pianos used for same purpose
$150.00

Lot of Oats taken by the troops encamped on my premises
$120.00

One Cow slaughtered by the troops
$50.00

Damage on Fruit and Ornamental Trees that were cut down $300.00

Damage to Dwelling
$200.00

Total amount of loss
$1920.00

Col. A. Matzdorff, Post Commander will testify as to the correctness of the losses sustained by me and also to my loyalty to the Government of the United States. Hoping you will lend me your aid in having my claims presented and audited for settlement. I have the honor General to remain,

Most respectfully your humble servant,

Albert Lotz

~

Hd. Qtrs. U.S. Forces

Franklin, TN. March 21, 1965

I hereby certify that the losses on property as stated by Mr. Albert Lotz are true, the breastworks and references of our forces at the battle of Franklin were on or in the immediate view of the premises of Mr. Lotz. It gives me pleasure to pronounce Mr. Lotz a most exemplary citizen, who never faltered in his devotion to the Union.

A. Matzdorff
Lient. Col. 75th Pa. Inf.
Comd'g Post

David Lotz states from family history that Albert was involved with the Underground Railroad – an organization that helped slaves escape to the North. His outward appearance was that of being neutral and wanting the country to be one nation. Mr. Lotz, who lives in

California, continues, "Economic depression followed the Civil War. People were not buying pianos. Albert was able to earn a living by making furniture and tuning various musical instruments. The Columbia Athenaeum of Columbia, TN provided him some employment. They gave Albert excellent recommendations, commending him for his fine work."

Some of his furniture found places of prestige – in the Franklin Courthouse and the Legion of Honor. He built several music stands, some of which are still in the Lotz family generations later. His apparent neutral political ideology caused him problems in the years following the war. Family lore states that he carved an eagle holding the flags of the Union and Confederate Armies on a piano he had built. This was to symbolize a new, unified country. His work did not sit well with the Ku Klux Klan of the area. The story goes he heard that the Klan planned to tar and feather him. With that, Albert left Franklin, sold his beautiful home and moved his family out of town.

From U.S. Patent #96710, dated, November 9, 1869, Franklin, TN we see that Albert Lotz was not only a master carpenter, but also a creator and designer. He invented what was entitled, "Improved Fire-Ladder." From the patent record: "Be it known that I, Albert Lotz, of Franklin, in the county of Williamson, and State of Tennessee, have invented certain new and useful improvements in the 'Saving-Apparatus;' and I do hereby declare that the following is a full, clear and exact description.... The nature of my invention consists in the construction and arrangement of an 'apparatus for saving life and property,' in case of fire, where the door or entrance to the house cannot be used...." It would appear that this fire escape slide patent arrived in the mail just about the time the Lotz' were preparing to leave Franklin.

Lotz move to California

At the end of 1869 or the early part of January, 1870 Albert and Margaret decided to move their family to California. It is unclear the route they took, but it is believed they may have first moved to Memphis, Tennessee, then on to San Jose, California. Albert was 49 years of age. The US Census records show their presence in San Jose, CA on July 14, 1870. Their Santa Clara County land deed states that Margaret Lotz purchased property in Block 63, Lot 8 (684 Second St.) on April 2, 1870 for $600 gold. Within a short time they added Lot 5, all in Reeds Addition. This property was sold by the family following Margaret's death on March 7, 1904. Later, Albert moved to 116 North 9th St. to live with his son, Joseph. After moving to San Jose, Albert continued his trade of making and tuning pianos along with the manufacture of carriages. His son Joseph arrived in February 1871 joining his dad in business. Joseph did the painting and finish work on both the carriages and pianos.

It appears that Margaret kept the household organized and the children involved in their artistic pursuits. She did find time to participate, along with Paul and Matilda, in demonstrating their creativity at the Santa Clara Valley County Fair in 1872. Listed under the Special Premium Awards we find "Mrs. M. Lotz - Seed-flower wreath, Hon. Mention" and under "Embroidery, Needle Work – Bead Work, Diploma." It appears the children were not the only creative ones in the family.

Margareta died on Nov 16, 1898 in San Jose. Following her death, Albert moved to San Francisco to live with his daughter, Amelia Lotz Ahlers. The 1900 US Census shows Albert living in the Ahlers home on June 7, at 1100 Eddy. A few months before his death, which came on November 11, 1905, Albert moved back to San Jose to live with his son, Joseph. At his death he was living at 116 South 9th St. The *San Jose Mercury* obituary stated, "The services were brief, and conducted by Rev. Mr. Meyer of the Oakland German Methodist Church, in the absence of the local minister. Mr. Lotz was a native of Germany, 85 years of age, and had lived in this vicinity nearly his entire life. He was one of the most respected and well known of the older residents of this city and had scores of friends throughout the county and San Francisco. Once known to a person Mr. Lotz never lost his friendship throughout his life."

Margaret and Albert are buried side by side at the Oak Hill Cemetery in San Jose. Their burial location is in Section AA, Lot 145, grave 1 & 2.

Joseph Albert Lotz

Joseph Lotz was an intelligent, gifted individual. He left home early, moving north from Tennessee. He was 20 years of age when the Civil War broke out. Joseph seemed to follow his parents' lead and stayed neutral throughout the war. In the early 1870s he was off for new opportunities in California. Within a few years he entered the local political arena where he would spend most of his adult life.

Joseph was born in Saxony, Germany, December 25, 1841. Joseph's mother, Margareta (Margaret) along with his sister, Amelia, came to America, probably in the late 1840s. Margaret was escaping from an abusive marriage. Joseph would have been eight to ten years of age when they arrived in the New Orleans, Louisiana area. Sometime around 1850 Margaret met Johann Albert Lotz. They were probably married in south Louisiana or the Mobile, Alabama area. No record has been found for their marriage. As an adult Joseph seemed reluctant to claim his German heritage. In most census or written articles he stated he was born in Louisiana or Tennessee. Some of this feeling probably came from the negative measures toward Germans during World War I and possibly his own personal feelings from difficult times as a child in Germany. From the 1880 US census, his parents stated Joseph and his sister were both born in Germany. In the

1860 and 1870 census when Joseph was not living at home, Amelia was listed as being born in Germany.

In the early 1850s the family moved north to Covington, KY, then to Warren County Ohio. In about 1854 they moved to Nashville. By 1855 they were in Franklin, TN. Joseph received his education in Nashville, graduating with honors from the public schools in June 1864. Shortly thereafter he left Tennessee to be on his own. Over the next few years, following the Civil War, he lived for short periods in Louisville, KY, Cincinnati, OH and Indianapolis, IN. He subsequently moved to Anderson, Madison County, IN and acquired the trade of carriage painter. All of this information comes from an article written in an 1881 book entitled, *History of Santa Clara County, CA.* No record can be found showing that Joseph served for either the north or south during the Civil War.

Joseph Joins Family in San Jose

Joseph's parents, Albert and Margaret, left Tennessee with his two brothers and two sisters, arriving in San Jose, CA in 1870. The family was united in February of 1871 when Joseph moved west and settled in San Jose. Joseph worked as a carriage painter and helped with the finishing work on pianos for his father. The San Jose City Directory for 1871-72 lists Albert Lotz, piano maker and Joseph Lotz, painter, both living at 684 Second St. Joseph joined his first civic club, the Painters Association of San Jose, in June 1872. From the June 5, *Daily Alta California*, a San Francisco newspaper we read, "A meeting of eight hour painters was held Saturday evening and organized as follows: ....Secretary, J. A. Lotz." In March of 1876 Joseph was appointed by the Mayor and Common Council for the city of San Jose to fill an unexpired term, as City Treasurer. In April he was elected to the permanent office of City Treasurer and continued in that position for the next six years. He then became the Santa Clara Deputy County Treasurer for the next eight years. He was then elected County Treasure and served faithfully until around 1909. Joseph ran for office in 1910 but apparently did not win.

Before being appointed City Treasurer there was a flurry of joining civic clubs. He was elected secretary of the Painters Association in June of 1872, and then on November 14, 1872 Joseph was elected secretary of the Board of Fire Delegates. In March 1873 Joseph was appointed by the Garden City Odd Fellows (IOOF) Lodge No. 142 to help organize the 54th anniversary of the Odd Fellows. In June 1875 Joseph was elected a Trustee of the same Lodge. It was apparent Joseph was making a name for himself in the community.

Joseph and Mamie Marry

A most interesting article was published in the *San Jose Mercury News* on May 10, 1887. It was entitled, "A sudden Departure, Mysterious Disappearance of Deputy Treasure J. A. Lotz." "Joseph A. Lotz has occupied the trusted position of Deputy County Treasurer for several years. He was formerly City Treasure and filled the office with ability. His integrity has never been questioned and he has always been regarded as one to the best citizens of San Jose. For the past few weeks the intimate friends of Mr. Lotz have noticed a slight change in his manner. He has had at times a dreamy far-away look in his eyes. He has had a habit of late of taking long walks in the early morning.....Of late I have noticed a change in him. He seemed nervous. At times I would speak to him and he would start suddenly as though awakened from a dream. Yesterday afternoon, just before we were closing the office Lotz said to me that he would like to take a vacation. This struck me as peculiar as he never cared to leave the office. To my surprise he became very much excited and said he must go today and he could not stay in San Jose another day. The young man was very pale. I became alarmed and told him to tell me everything, that I was his friend and would help him. I said to him, go on, let me hear the worst. He told me he was going to get married. He stated he was going to get married in Sacramento tomorrow to Miss Cross a young lady from that city. Mr. Lotz has the best wishes of a host of friends in San Jose who would have extended congratulations had the opportunity been offered." (This article has been condensed from the fifteen paragraph article.)

Joseph and Mamie Cross were married in the Sacramento, CA area on May 11, 1887. From the *Sacramento Daily Union* , dated May 14, 1887, "Miss Mamie Cross, of this city, and J. A. Lotz a prominent citizen of San Jose were united in marriage in this city last Wednesday at the residence of the bride's sister, Mrs. Simeon Brown, Rev. A. C. Herrick officiating. After the ceremony and congratulations, the party adjourned to the dining room and partook of a fine wedding breakfast. The presents were mostly silverware. Among them was an elegant silver tea service, presented by a sister of the bridegroom in San Jose. (It is interesting to note that Joseph's sister, Matilda was living in San Francisco, having recently arrived from Europe.) The happy couple departed on the train for San Francisco, where they will remain till the 24th, when they will sail for Honolulu with the Masonic excursion. When they return they will reside in San Jose." Mamie's mother was Lizzie Cross Peckham. She died Jul 30, 1915 in Oakland and is buried in the Mountain View Cemetery next to Joseph and Mamie.

On May 24, 1887 an article came out in the *San Jose Mercury News* entitled, "Going to the Islands, San Joseans start on an Ocean Steamer Excursion this Afternoon." "The Oceanic steamer, Australia of the Spreckels line left San Francisco this afternoon at 2 o'clock, with a large party of Mason excursionists on board, bound for Honolulu. Every berth was taken and the passengers number 110 adults and a dozen children. The following named San Joseans were among the passengers: Joseph A. Lotz and wife...."

Political career covers 33 years

Joseph Lotz was very involved in the Republican Party. From age 35 in 1876 to age 68 in 1909, a span of 33 years, he held public office. During that time he was appointed Treasure then elected to the office for the City of San Jose. He then was appointed Deputy Treasure and elected Treasure for Santa Clara County. Over the years he found himself involved in many important issues as a representative of his city and county. One such high profile issue was initiated on December 22, 1893, when he felt compelled to file suit on behalf of the county against the trustees of Leland Stanford, Jr. University and Jane Lathrop Stanford as the executrix of the will of her husband, Leland Stanford. Seems the state had passed a law providing that a tax of $5 on every $100 could be levied on all inheritances, save those made to immediate blood relatives. The law went on to say that it should be the responsibility of the County Treasurer to collect the tax and turn it over to the State school fund. Santa Clara County and Treasurer Lotz lost the case mainly on the grounds that Leland Stanford lived and died in San Francisco, which is out of the county's jurisdiction. Stanford was a former

Governor and Senator from California. He and his wife, Jane, had just created a university and named it after their recently diseased son. Yes, this was the preeminent Stanford University.

In that same year Joseph Lotz made the headlines in the *San Francisco Chronicle* on November 14, 1893. "County Treasurer, Joseph A. Lotz had an experience with a supposed burglar Thursday evening and has not yet recovered his feeling of security. The fact that he is the only one who works the combination on the big vault where Santa Clara County's money is kept is not only known to the residents of this town, but to the professional safe-crackers, and consequently he was picked out by burglars as he right man to go to." The article goes on to say, "Lotz had heard about a robbery of the Treasurer at Healdsburg and had armed himself with a pistol. It seems he had returned home to his residence at 46 N. Eighth St. In a short time a man came to the door telling Mrs. Lotz he wanted to speak to her husband. 'I want to see you privately,' said the man. Feeling this could be a problem Mr. Lotz would not be coaxed outside. The man left limping but was seen later with his partner walking just fine. The next day the same two men were seen hanging around Lotz house. Then the following day Mr. Lotz saw the men on First St. but before he could find an officer the men had disappeared."

Cyril C. Lotz is born

Joseph and Mamie were married thirty-four years. They had one child, Cyril Clyde Lotz, who was born on April 8, 1889 in San Jose. In adulthood Cyril became a well-known attorney in San Francisco and Oakland, CA. As a young boy Cyril was seen as a literary prodigy and as a young man was highlighted for his work as an amateur wireless telegrapher. On April 20, 1902, at the age of 12, he was featured in an article reviewing the book he had written called, "Stories for Children." The *San Francisco Call* stated that "he has attended the Washburn School for the past three years, with a literary bent and is just like other boys, with the exception that he would rather write stories than engage in the usual pastimes of his companions. He has been a lover of literature and has been constantly grinding out boyish stories. Many of these have been printed in the daily papers and this encouraged him."

It is interesting to note a few months later, on September 25, 1902 an article appeared in the *San Francisco Call* concerning Cyril being dangerously ill. It was entitled, "Boy Author Seriously Ill." "Roy Lotz who has gained some reputation as a boy author is dangerously ill at his home in this city (San Jose). Roy is but 13 years of age and has shown genius as a writer. Roy Lotz is said to be the youngest author of note in the State. He is the son of Joseph Lotz, the County Treasurer." This is the only reference the author has found of him being called Roy.

On April 20, 1909, Cyril petitioned the Common Council of San Jose, asking permission to use the electric tower for his aerial to help in the transmission for his wireless telegraphy station. Then on July 8, 1909, again, an article from the *San Jose Mercury News* states, "Cyril C. Lotz a young amateur wireless telegrapher living at 116 S. Ninth St. in this city has by the aid of his instruments been able to catch many of the government messages from their official stations and is so enthusiastic over his success that he will install a more efficient apparatus and with co-operation of the Bay Counties Wireless Telegraphers Association of which he is a member will engage in commercial business." Then on September 23, 1909, the News reported, "Youth is Holder of Wireless Record." "The world's amateur long distance wireless telegraphy record has been established by Cyril Lotz the 19 year old son of J. A. Lotz formerly county treasurer of Santa Clara County. The boy has just received word from several commercial wireless companies that his record talk with the United States steamship West Virginia, while the vessel was 2,800 miles south of San Francisco, has never been equaled by amateur operators."

On June 5, 1917, Cyril filed for his draft registration card in San Francisco at age 26. He had just married Dorothea Russell. It states that he was an Attorney at Law, and that he was unable to serve because of his physical disability and his dependency on his wife. Written on the card is a rejection for physical disability by the 12th Naval Reserve, Radio Division, June 4, 1917.

The *San Jose Mercury News*, February 20, 1917, states that a Sunday wedding was held for Cyril C. Lotz, a law clerk in Los Angeles, and Miss Dorothea Lucile Russell at the Congregational Church. The 1930 U.S. Census it shows that they had three children, Cyril C. Jr., Joseph Earl and David L. Lotz.

Joseph and Mamie move to Berkeley

During their married years, Joseph and Mamie lived in San Jose at 116 S. 9th. In about 1920, they moved to Berkeley, Alameda County, CA to live close to their son, Cyril. They resided at 2428 Roosevelt Ave.

During the early 1900s, Joseph went into business with son, Cyril. It appears they were partners with a man named, L. H. Lewars. The business was located in Berkeley and named Hygienic Health Food Company. From an Oakland paper in 1920, it states Lewars was president, Cyril C. Lotz, secretary and J.A. Lotz was a director.

Mamie died on August 18, 1921 at the St. Helena sanitarium in Napa County. She was an author of both prose and verso compositions. Voter registration records in 1924 show Cyril, Dorothy and Joseph lived at 1933 El Dorado Ave. in Berkeley. Joseph died at age 83 in Berkeley on July 15, 1925. Both Joseph and Mamie are buried in Mountain View Cemetery in Alameda, CA.

As mentioned before, Joseph was an active member of several civic groups in San Jose. He was secretary of the Volunteer Fire Department from 1872 to 1876. On July 6, 1876 he was elected into the Masonic membership of Friendship Lodge No. 210. He was elected to the office of Worshipful Master for 1880-'81. In 1901, he was initiated into the Elks Lodge. One would think his early involvement in so many fraternal organizations may have helped in his election to public office.

On September 25, 1894 an article ran in the *San Jose Mercury News* promoting Joseph A. Lotz's upcoming election. "If there is one office in the county that demands a custodian of unflinching integrity it is that of county treasurer. For near a quarter of a century Joseph A. Lotz has occupied positions of trust in this community, and during the whole of that time he has demonstrated his superior capacity and has secured the unlimited confidence and esteem of the people he has served. ......The present county treasurer has achieved a high popularity for his obliging disposition, the modesty of his demeanor and the intelligence and promptness with which he has discharged all duties during his long career of public service, a popularity which will be attested by the voters early in November." How would you not vote for the man!

Amelia Lotz Ahlers

Amelia Lotz was the oldest child at home during the Battle of Franklin. She was a young woman of 17, who undoubtedly carried heavy responsibility for the younger children of the family. From the very beginning she showed amazing musical talent. Amelia learned to play the piano on an instrument built by her own father. She was enrolled in the music scholars program in Franklin, building on the skills she had learned at home. Family lore indicates Amelia grew to become a concert pianist, although no substantiating facts have been found to prove the story. As a married woman living in San Francisco, Amelia seemed to be in the shadow of her husband, Henry Ahlers, much of the time. This prominent couple became a part of the social fiber of San Francisco society.

It is believed that Amelia Lotz was born May 8, 1847, in Saxony, Germany. Her birth date listed on different documents changed several times over the years. After her marriage, she always remained a few years younger than her husband. Reality is, Amelia and her brother, Joseph were born in Germany, coming to America with their mother. Her death certificate states she was born in Mobile, AL, while three of the federal census records state she was born in Louisiana. The information given on two of her daughter's death certificates state she was born in Louisiana. As long as Amelia was living with her parents, the census (1860-1870) stated she was born in Saxony, Germany. The 1860 census says she was 13 years old on June 10, which makes her birth, 1847. She was the oldest child living at home in Franklin, TN in 1860.

Her mother was Margareta (Margaret) Grass (Grasz.) Her father is unknown. Family history states that Amelia, Joseph and their mother came to America, with Margareta escaping an abusive marriage. After arriving in America it appears they were living in the New Orleans, LA area, possibly in or near Mobile, AL. Margareta and her children would have immigrated after 1847 but before the early 1850's when she and Albert Lotz probably married. It is believed Margareta and Albert Lotz met in the New Orleans area. The family lived in Covington, KY near Cincinnati, Warren County, OH and Nashville, TN before moving to Franklin, TN in about May of 1855.

On January 28, 1862, Amelia is recorded as one of the students enrolled at the Franklin Female Institute near Five Points in downtown Franklin, TN. The list contained children who were scholars and music scholars. It is very possible that Amelia began her studies in piano at a very young age at the Franklin Female Institute. Amelia was 17 years old when the Battle of Franklin took place. One can imagine the responsibility she would have held while taking care of her younger brothers and sister during those hours of the battle.

In 1869, the family left Franklin and migrated to San Jose, CA. The census records state that as a young adult Amelia was a piano teacher. On January 18, 1882, Amelia Lotz and Henry C. Ahlers were married in San Jose. Henry operated a jewelry business. In a newspaper ad that ran in the *San Jose Mercury News*, dated March 6, 1886, it states, "Henry C. Ahlers, The Leading Jeweler and Diamond Dealer – upstairs, over First National Bank." Another ad, December 3, 1886, states, "Christmas at Ahler's – The holidays are approaching and Henry C. Ahlers can show you the best selection of diamonds and diamond jewelry in every conceivable design. …The only jewelry house in San Jose which keeps no plated goods of any kind. Open evenings until Jan. 1, 1887."

From the *San Jose Mercury*, November 28, 1917, from an article entitled "25 Years Ago Today:" "Henry C. Ahlers, for many years a leading jewelry dealer of this city has opened a first-class store at No. 7 Kearny St., San Francisco." That would mean the Ahlers family moved to San Francisco in 1892. All their children were born in San Jose.

The Ahlers Children

Lillian Margaret Ahlers was born, November 28, 1882; Amelia was born in September 1886; Viola Evelyn, born September 15, 1889; and their youngest daughter, Blanche A. Ahlers, was born April 24, 1890. A son named Henry G. Ahlers died at 14 days old. He was born on May 22, 1884. No record has been found for daughter Amelia living to adulthood. She may have died soon after her birth in 1886. Lillian was never married and was living in her mom's home (3876 Clay) at the time of her death, April 25, 1961. When Amelia died in 1940 she and Lillian were living together.

Viola Evelyn married John Louis Whelan in about 1909. Viola provided the informant information for her sisters, Blanche and Lillian's death certificates. At the time of Viola's death, she owned a large collection of Matilda Lotz's art. John Whelan died July 31, 1941, and Viola died December 30, 1969.

Blanche A. Lotz married Terry Wilson Ward on February 18, 1919. She died December 2, 1961. It appears that all the members of this Ahlers family lived in San Francisco. Henry, Amelia and all their children are buried at the Oak Hill Cemetery in San Jose. John Whelan, Viola's husband, is also buried there. They are all in Section I, Block 232, Lot 3.

Some interesting notes concerning three of the daughters are available. Lillian graduated from the San Francisco Girls High School on June 4, 1901. As a single person at age 34, she was involved in organizing a benefit to raise money for the auxiliary of the Girls Befriending Society.

Viola graduated from the John Swett Grammar School on June 15, 1900. Viola Ahlers was one of six students who received a special medal. Then sadly, on May 9, 1908, an article with a headline, "Five Prominent Students at the University Said to Have 'Cribbed'." It seems that Viola was one of the girls that was not going to be allowed to graduate from the University of California with her class because of a charge brought from one of their professors. Viola, who was a member of the Phi Bata Kappa sorority in Berkeley, in fact did have enough credits to graduate. Seems the campus was divided over the affair. The good news was that on January 5, 1911, Viola received her high school teaching certificate from the San Francisco School System. Viola and her husband, John Whelan had four children: Margaret E. b. 1915, Jane B. b. 1917, John L. b. 1920 and Marie L. b. 1922.

Blanche attended California State University. From an article in the *San Francisco Chronicle*, dated May 2, 1911, we read the headline, "Baby Dolls Do Not Like Scene." Seems Blance Ahlers and a number of other girls struck the play, saying they would not fall into the arms of male chorus men at the conclusion of the dance. The girls claim they were asked to wear short dresses and the proposed familiarity was altogether lacking in dignity. The article went on to say, "the feature will be dropped for the present unless the coach is able to bring the men and women of the chorus closer together." Things turned out well for Blanche. She was married to Terry Wilson in 1919 when 200 people were invited to the wedding, which was held at the home of her parents. Prior to the wedding a tea was given in her honor by Blanche's sister, Mrs. John Whelan. The June 26, 1928, passenger list of the ship *America* shows Blanche and her husband, Terry returning on a trip to France. Traveling with them were two of Terry's family members, Elisa Scott Ward, age 79, and Russella Scott Ward, age 81.

The Ups and Downs of Henry's Business

The *San Jose Mercury News* for August 11, 1894, reported that "Henry C. Ahlers, formerly engaged in business in this city, went to San Francisco about two years ago. …His creditors have recently taken charge of the business and find that of $28,000 which he owes for stock, there will be but about half the amount for the creditors." By November 28, 1894, Henry had moved his jewelry business to 126 Kearny St., Room 27, upstairs. Amelia's, Henry seemed to always use the middle letter C. to distinguish himself from another Henry Ahlers who lived and worked in San Francisco.

In March of 1904, a man named Louis Pacheco was charged with grand larceny. Seems that the robber ran out of Ahlers Jewelers with diamonds from the showcase in order to give a diamond ring to the girl he expected to marry. He was captured after a hot chase by Henry and another jeweler friend. On January 15, 1907, the *Evening News* of San Jose states that "H. C. Ahlers a jeweler, who deals in diamonds and precious stones at 1460 Sutter St., San Francisco grappled with a thief, wrestled the revolver from his hand and had the satisfaction, a few minutes later, of delivering the would-be robber to the police." On the same day, The *San Francisco Call* paper displayed more than a half-page article concerning the event, with photos of Ahlers and the robber. It appears not only was he very able physically, but Henry must also have recovered very nicely from his 1894 business problems.

Ahler's a Trotting Horse Breeder

Just before the turn of the century, articles concerning the Ahlers family began to show up in the *San Francisco Chronicle's* horse racing page. The first such article appeared on April 30, 1898. "H. C. Ahlers won 1ˢᵗ place by driving his trotter, La Trappe at Ingleside Race Track." In August 1904, he was active in the Pacific Coast Trotting Horse Breeders Association and was scheduled to drive his horse, named Telephone. On March 9, 1913, Henry purchased Matawan, the big trotting horse from I. L. Borden. The paper states, "Matawan was recently gelded and good results are expected. Ahlers will race his new trotting acquisition at the matinees at the park this coming season."

Then in May of 1913, a three-column photo of Henry racing appeared in the *Chronicle*. Under the photo it states, "H. C. Ahlers driving Matawan to victory over Merrylina in the second and deciding heat of free-for-all trot." The pressure must have been on to prove the worth of his new trotter, because on December 29, 1913, an article appeared stating, "H. C. Ahlers and T. D. Sexton indulged in an argument the other night at the horse sale regarding the relative merits of Matawan and Silver Hunter with the result that a match race has been arranged between the two trotters. Two hundred and fifty dollars a side will be put up and it is understood that Ahlers will drive Matawan and Sexton will be behind Silver Hunter. Both horses have raced on the California circuit but of late have been entertaining the crowds at the stadium. It is hoped that the match will be staged at the Speedway so that everyone will get a chance to see the contest."

In the spring of 1916 there was a large photo in the *Chronicle* society page showing an attractive young lady riding a horse. The caption said, "Miss Margaret Robertson will take part in the society horse show that is being planned for the latter part of the month at the San Francisco Riding Club. She is here photographed on H. C. Ahlers three-year old champion, Mavis in Golden Gate Park." It appears Henry had moved into saddle horses and was doing very well for himself. On May 4, 1919, an article was printed with the headline, "H. C. Ahlers Mare, Mavis Wins Coast Saddle Horse Championship Ribbon." It goes on to say, "Santa Barbara's first annual horse show came to a successful close tonight with a ball in the main lobby of the Belvedere....The saddle horse class for animals over 15-2 hands brought out a score of fine entries. In the end, Mavis, owned by Hanry C. Ahlers of San Francisco, was given the blue ribbon thereby giving the mare the distinction of being the champion Kentucky saddle equine of the Pacific Coast."

Amelia Joins Her Husband in Horse Racing

Then on September 5, 1919, an article appeared in the *Chronicle* datelined, Sacramento, CA "Fairmark Governors Day. The horse shows are attracting a great deal of attention nightly at the State Fair." Then under a sub-head, "Saddle Horse Award, High-stepper prize winners were: First, San Vicenie, Mrs. H. C. Ahlers….." It now appears Amelia Lotz Ahlers is into the horse show business with her husband. Also at the Sacramento State Fair on the 13th of September, the paper reported, "Two saddle horses, owned by H. C. Ahlers of San Francisco, won the highest honors at the State Fair in the competition that came to a close the fore part of the week. Sam Vicente, a beautiful 6 year-old chestnut stallion, for the third year in succession came home unbeaten in the five gaited saddle classes at the fair. Vicente won ten first prizes, including the championship for five-gaited saddle horses and the grand championship for stallions, in the breeding classes for American saddle horses. Mavis, a mare owned by Ahlers, and purchased during the exposition won six prizes, including the championship for three-gaited saddle horses and the grand championship for mares in the breeding classes for American saddle horses. This is a record for two horses belonging to one owner quite likely to stand for some time."

As late as October 1921, Henry is still showing horses at age 64. H. C. Ahlers is listed with his famous stallion, Bruce McDonald, at the California National Live Stock Association in San Francisco.

During the years the Ahlers were in San Francisco they lived in the following residences: 1892 to 1906 - 1102 Eddy. Then, for a short time after the 1906 earthquake, they remained at the Eddy address. Then from 1908 to 1913 they lived at 1985 Oak. In the City Directory for 1914, it appears they moved for a third time to 2300 Divisadero. By 1920, the Ahlers had moved to 3876 Clay. Amelia was still living in the Clay street home when she died on December 13, 1940, at age 93.

Henry was born in Germany on January 19, 1857, and died in San Francisco, CA on June 1, 1935. He is buried next to his wife, Amelia, in the Oak Hill Cemetery, San Jose, CA. In his will dated August 8, 1930, Henry left half of his estate to his wife, Amelia. The other half of his estate was left to his three daughters, Lillian M. Ahlers, Viola Whelan and Blanche Ward. Viola and Blanch were co-executors. Henry had $57,000 in stocks and shares and a home worth $7,000, which he had transferred to his three daughters.

Paul Lotz

It is easy to imagine Paul outside on a summer day in Franklin, TN drawing a picture in the dirt for his younger sister, Matilda. Neither had any idea how the next few years would turn their world upside down, but at the same time would help teach them to survive life's difficulties. There is no question that Paul and his younger sister Matilda had a special bond that would last for the rest of their lives. On that epic day in April 1906 when the earth shook in northern California, Paul's prosperous and secure life would change forever. One could imagine the thankfulness he felt knowing his sister, Matilda was far away, safe in Europe.

Paul Lotz was born on February 23, 1855, in Nashville, TN. We know the Albert Lotz family first arrived in Nashville before moving on to Franklin in about May of 1855. The oldest son, Joseph, indicated through an article written in 1888 that the family moved to Nashville in about 1854. U.S. Census records for 1860 and 1870 indicated Paul's birth as 1855. In the years following, the census always shows him at a younger age than his true age. In his passport application in 1900, Paul indicates his birth date is February 23, 1862. He died in New York City of a heart attack on September 20, 1913, at age 58.

Paul was the first child born to Albert and Margareta Lotz. He had an older stepsister, Amelia and a stepbrother,

Joseph. Margareta was married and living in Germany when she gave birth to Amelia and Joseph before migrating to America. While living in Franklin, Matilda, Julie and Julius (twins) and Augustus were all born. Julie and Julius tragically died in early 1864. Paul was nine years old when the family made that historic walk to The Carter House for safety during the Battle of Franklin, November 30, 1864.

When he was fourteen the family made the move to San Jose, California. In his early years he developed into yet another artistic Lotz child. From the *San Francisco Bulletin* dated, October 2, 1873, we read, "Santa Clara Valley Fair – Paul Lotz, a youth of sixteen, (true age 18) has crayon drawings and a two-story bird cage of elaborate workmanship. The design, which is very beautiful, is said to be his own. Also, Matilda Lotz has a specimen of wood carving, a deer, finely executed." It was reported in the full report of the Santa Clara Valley Agricultural Society that Paul's Lotz's Bird Cage received an honorable mention and special note: "For which the committee urged a special premium, as they believed it to be among the most meritorious and elegant objects of the exhibition." It is believed that Paul had a strong influence on his sister Matilda, helping her learn to draw during their childhood. At age 16, on December 27, 1871, Paul executed a pen drawing of a school-house for which he was listed on the Grand Roll of Honor for the First Grammar Department of the Santa Clara-Street School.

In the *San Jose City Directory* for 1878, Paul is listed as an artist for what is believed to be a photography studio owned by W. W. Wright. In that same year he moves to nearby San Francisco and goes to work as a photographer for a Joseph T. Silva. The next year, 1879, he establishes himself as a retoucher for the man who will one day become his photographic business partner, Thomas H. Jones. Thomas H. Jones & Co. was located at 838 Market. As early as 1879, the business was also called Elite Photographic Gallery. In 1880 the business had become Jones, Robinson & Co. Jones had two partners, Alexander Robertson and George M. Robinson. Paul continued to work as a retoucher until August 8, 1883, when the San Francisco Chronicle announced, "T. H. Jones of the celebrated Elite Photograph Studio, 838 Market St. has formed a co-partnership with Paul Lotz the well known photographic artist." For many years they seemed to go by both, Jones & Lotz and Elite Photographic Gallery.

In 1878, Paul and his sister Matilda moved to San Francisco where she enrolled in the California School of Design. She and Paul both rented rooms at 1025 Lombard. The next year, 1879, they changed addresses and moved to 4 Highland Terrace. In the 1880 U.S. Census Paul is listed as living at 838 Market St., San Francisco, which is also where he was employed as a Photographic Artist. Matilda continued to live at the Highland Terrace address until she graduated and moved to Paris. The City Directories indicate that Paul lived in several different locations, 1885 - 236 Taylor, 1887 - 209 Hyde. It is interesting to note that Matilda had been in Europe studying and painting from 1880 until she returned in October, 1886. She then resided at the Hyde address, near Paul until her return to Europe in August of 1888.

On July 17, 1884, the *San Francisco Chronicle* carried an advertisement headed, "FLOODED, Hanly's Commercial Mart, along with a letter from The Elite Photograph Gallery," "from Messrs, Jones & Lotz, July 14, 1884, Dear Sir: The damage caused to you by the overflow of water from our Parlors, through the negligence of one of our employees, has been estimated at $14,000, and judged a fair valuation by the appraisers mutually appointed by us. Of course, we are sorry that such an accident should occur. You will find inclosed a cheque for the amount. Yours truly, Jones & Lotz." The rest of the article is a list of damaged items up for sale. The addresses were 834, 836 and 838 Market St.

In the "Arts and Artists" article from the *San Francisco Chronicle*, dated July 14, 1889, we read, "Paul Lotz has gone to Paris to join his sister, Miss Matilda Lotz, who is filling orders there." It goes on to speculate, "It is probable that the two will return in a few months." It is very likely Paul came home by himself.

In a newsworthy article dated March 29, 1893, we read: "SAFE CRACKERS, Burglars Make a Good Haul in a Studio. Safecrackers are again at work. On Monday night they made a rich haul from the safe in the Elite Photograph Studio, 838 Market St., between Grant Ave. and Stockton St. The detectives have little to say about the case, because they no doubt suspect that the job was done by some person or persons familiar with the methods of T. H. Jones and Paul Lotz, the proprietors..... With a small but stiff piece of metal the tumblers in the old lock were turned over and the door opened. After taking the $500, all in good, hard money, the thieves decamped as quietly as they had entered."

In the early part of 1898, Paul Lotz became the new owner of the Elite Photographic Studio. It continued operation at 838 Market. He apparently had bought out Thomas H. Jones. At this point, Paul seemed to have everything going his way. He moved his residence to 313 Leavenworth in 1899, then to 203 Tuck St. in 1900. Paul filed for a passport application in San Francisco on July 8, 1900. On September 12, 1900, Paul Lotz was listed in the *Oakland Tribune*, along with several other Californians who were to participate in the Paris World's Fair Exposition, which ran from April 15 to November 12, 1900. In his passport application we get a clearer view of what he looked like. He was 5 foot 8 ½ inches, broad forehead, gray eyes, large nose and mouth, broad square chin, brown hair, with long face and fair complexion.

The headline dated December 4, 1901, from the *San Francisco Chronicle* read, "Bad Investment for Lotz, Photograph Gallery at Presidio Brought Him No Profit." It seems Paul had committed $3,000 toward a half interest in a concession that would include a photograph gallery in the upscale Presidio area. He had paid $1,500 and written two notes for $500 each. It came out in the Superior Court that "fraud had been practiced on Mr. Lotz by a J. D. Givins. ....But as Lotz continued to operate under his agreement with Givins after learning of the fraud, he would have to bear his liability on the note." Paul was out at least $500 and probably more.

"The beginning of the unparalleled catastrophe was on the morning of April 18, 1906. In the grey dawn, when but few had arisen for the day, a shock of earthquake rocked the foundations of the city and precipitated scenes of panic and terror throughout the business and residence districts. After four days and three nights that have no parallel outside of Dante's Inferno, the city of San Francisco, the American metropolis by the Golden Gate, was a mass of glowing embers fast resolving into heaps and windrows of grey ashes emblematic of devastation and death."

These words come from the first pages of the classic book, *Complete Story of San Francisco Horror*, written by Hubert D. Russell, published in 1906. This firsthand account reminds us of how difficult it must have been for the Lotz family. Every indication tells us that they were all there to experience the horror and devastation. Amelia and her husband Henry C. Ahlers, a prominent jeweler and horse breeder, as well as Augustus, now married with three beautiful daughters, were all living in the doomed city.

From family legend we learn Augustus lost his manufacturing business. Paul, now 51 years of age, lost everything including his prominent business on Market Street. Matilda, the famous animal painter would soon be worrying about her family while painting in Europe. What a tragedy this must have been in all their lives.

Just 10 days following the earthquake and fire, we read from the *San Francisco Chronicle*, "Where People Can Be

Found, List of those who Escaped From the City Just After the Earthquake. The *Chronicle* prints below a list of people, with their present addresses, who registered at the bureau established at the Ferry depot and elsewhere on the day of the disaster." On the list: "Lotz, Paul, 2424 Gough." From all accounts, Paul Lotz had lost everything. In 1907 and 1908 neither Paul nor Augustus are listed in the city directory. In 1909 and 1910 Paul is a border in a rooming house at 1916 Eddy. He was listed as a photograper but the business, Elite Photograph Studio, was no more.

One report from the 1907 *Wilson's Photographic Magazine*, Vol. 44 indicates Paul stayed active in the community during the San Francisco recovery. "Report of the Relief Committee of the Photographers' Association of California. The purpose of the Relief Fund is to receive money and contributions of any kind from any persons or association for the benefit of such photographers of San Francisco, and State of California generally, who lost their all, place of business or had otherwise suffered by the great disaster of April 18, 1906.

The Relief Committee of the Photographers' Association of California consisted of the following active members: "O. H. Boye, Chairman; ....Paul Lotz, Treasurer." It is interesting to note that Paul wrote the report for the trade magazine and indicated the total cash contributions for the relief fund was nearly three thousand dollars, most of which was donated by the photographers of New York City, the State of New York and the Boston area. One could speculate that this may have been the door that opened for him and was the motivation to later move to New York City.

Paul was single all his life. But on August 13, 1909, a *San Francisco Call* newspaper the headline read – "Deed of Gift was Void rules Judge – Mrs. Coffey's conveyance of $6,000 to fiancé set aside." It goes on to say: "An attempt made in 1902 by Mrs. Mary F. Coffey to make a deed of gift of everything she possessed to Paul Lotz, a photographer to whom she was engaged to be married was defeated, a decision rendered by Judge Graham yesterday. Mrs. Coffey made an assignment to Lotz of two bank books representing deposits of a little more than $6,000 and also signed a deed of conveying to him two lots at the corner of Taylor and Pacific streets worth $12,000. The deeds were placed in escrow with her attorney, Fisher Ames, to be given to Lotz upon the death of Mrs. Coffey.

By putting the deeds in escrow she defeated her own purpose, according to Judge Graham's decision yesterday in a suite affecting the bank books. Although it was Mrs. Coffey's intention to make a gift to Lotz, she did not in actuality part with the possession of the books, the court held. The effect of the decision is that a daughter of Mrs. Coffey will get the money. The suit involving the validity of the deed of gift of land to Lotz has not been decided."

Then on February 18, 1910, the *San Francisco Call* ran an article entitled, "Coffey's Daughter Gets All of Mother's Estate – Gift of $15,000 to Paul Lotz is Declared Void." The article goes on to say, "Judge Graham yesterday refused a new trial in the case of John Farnham, the former public administrator, against Paul Lotz, and the result of the judgment is that Mrs. J. O'Day, daughter of attorney Joseph Coffey, inherits the $15,000 estate of her mother. Coffey's wife, after she was separated from the attorney by divorce, became acquainted with Paul Lotz a photographer, and placed her entire estate in the hands of Attorney Fisher Ames with directions that it be given to Lotz upon her death. She died in September, 1902. Judge Graham ruled that the attempt to give the money to Lotz was voided without effect."

In 1912, the city directory shows he was living as a border at 1499 Sutter. He continued to be listed as a photographer but with no business location.

Soon after this Paul Lotz left San Francisco and moved to Manhattan in New York City. His death certificate states that he was a photographer living in a hotel at 49 W. 27th. He had only lived in New York City for two years when he died of a heart attack. Paul's ashes were buried in his parents plot in the Oak Hill Cemetery in San Jose, CA on September 4, 1914. Below his parent's names the writing on the stone reads, "Paul Lotz, Died September 20, 1913." Joseph Lotz and Amelia Ahlers, Paul's brother and sister, were the appointed administrators for the estate. At his death, his total estate was valued at $7,410.28. Each of his four brothers and sisters received an equal share of his estate.

In San Francisco, Paul Lotz's life was recalled in the fall 1913 issue of *Camera Craft*, Vol. 20. "Paul Lotz, one of the best known photographers in this city, passed away in

New York on September twenty-first at the age of fifty-seven years. He was one of the most popular men in the profession, both here and throughout the East, on account of his most pleasing personality, kind disposition and sincere and upright character. Lovable to a degree, his death is mourned by all who had the good fortune to know him; and, as he took an active part in every movement for the betterment of photography, those so sorrowed make up no small number."

Matilda Lotz (Blaskovits)

Matilda was the second child of Albert and Margareta Lotz. She had a stepbrother and sister, Joseph and Amelia, both older. Her older brother Paul, during her younger Franklin years, became her mentor and supportive friend. They both carried responsibility for looking after their young brother, Augustus. In all, there were five children who grew to adulthood. From an early age, Matilda began to demonstrate creative abilities and a capacity and rapport to connect with animals in a special way. She was considered by many to be the most talented and successful of all the Lotz children. We can certainly say she was the most prominent and well known of all the children. She seemed to always portray herself with an independent spirit, which served her well and carried her to the far reaches of the world.

Matilda was born in Franklin, TN on November 29, 1858. She was the first child born in their new home on Columbia Pike. Albert completed construction of the home earlier that year. He moved his pregnant wife and family from their house in downtown Franklin to the five acres he had purchased from Fountain B. Carter. Matilda grew to be a woman that was ahead of her time. After years as a successful artist, world traveler and self-reliant individual, she married a well known European artist, Ferene (Ferencz) Blaskovits in Paris, 1913. She was 55 years of age. Matilda, a world renowned animal painter, died in Tata, Hungary on February 21, 1923.

November 29, 1864, the day before the historic Battle of Franklin, Matilda Lotz celebrated her sixth birthday. Little did they know the events following that fateful day would change the course of history for thousands of men and women as well as the Lotz's family.

Twenty years later on April 30, 1884, a foreign correspondent by the name of James H. Haynie, who was reporting for the *New Orleans Times Picayune* told a captivating story. Seems he and Matilda had met and began discussing their firsthand experiences from the Civil War. Haynie lived in Illinois and fought for the Union Army and young Matilda lived just south of Nashville where she experienced one of the bloodiest battles of the war. Haynie reports, "....when General George H. Thomas was maneuvering us against General Hood's brave army, we tramped and fought over pretty much all the roads and farms of that part of Middle Tennessee. One day, little Matilda Lotz sat on a rail fence and saw men and horses shot down all around her and she never flinched or cried; but when a stray bullet killed a pet calf and her mama told her 'twas the Yankees that did it,' she burst into tears and said that she hated us. She is just as brave and good today as she was then; chockfull of talent which finds vent in painting animals, and mark my prediction, some of us not yet out of our forties will live to see her name take rank with that of Rosa Bonheur's." This may well have been the life-changing event that captivated Matilda's love for animals and her desire to honor and preserve them with oil on canvas.

The Move to San Jose, California

In 1869, when Matilda was twelve, the family moved to San Jose, CA. One can imagine the hours that she and her brother Paul spent sketching the beauty of the landscape between Tennessee and California. They both showed signs of being very artistic at an early age. From the *San Francisco Bulletin*, October 2, 1873, "Santa Clara Valley Fair – Paul Lotz, a youth of sixteen, has crayon drawings and a two-story bird cage of elaborate workmanship. The design, which is very beautiful, is said to be his own. Also, Matilda Lotz has a specimen of wood carving, a deer, finely executed." At this same fair, Matilda offered a crayon drawing for which she received a $5 prize.

The Albert Lotz family was now well established and living in their two story home at 684 Second St.

Matilda always seemed to lean toward creating art from nature and especially animal life. Her brother Joseph said of her in the *Evening News*, San Jose, CA, August 2, 1917 "First little Matilda copied sheep. They were copies, but it is wonderful that a child could have done it at all. When she was only six years old she did her first original work. Today this painting, about ten by ten inches, in a little black walnut frame hangs on Mr. Lotz's wall. The picture shows Matilda Lotz's love for animals, for the steer's face shines with goodness." Being painted by the child at age six, one can believe that this may in fact be the pet calf that was killed by the "Yankees" back in Tennessee.

From a full page article in the *San Francisco Call*, December 8, 1901 the artist is remembered as follows: "The early education of this artist who portrays animal life with such realism was gleaned here, where in the schoolroom the little miss was at once the delight and despair of her teacher. Delight because she was so deliciously droll; despair because, like all artists, she refused point blank to cudgel her brain over the mathematical problem whether two or two made four or six. She preferred instead to draw. On every book and blank leaf, every piece of paper was pictures-landscapes, houses, cows, horses -anything and everything in the way of pictures, but her pet subject seemed to be pigs. On the margin of her arithmetic all around the pictures of the village blacksmith in the Second Reader, were pigs – whole processions of them....and other animals too, some of them entirely unknown to the world of science, strange looking creatures but all in proportion were drawn."

Later, when her mother began to add inches to the length of her skirt and she tied blue ribbons on her dignified marguerite braids, her chief delight was to visit the zoo. The old Woodward Gardens was a favorite resort and there she sketched lions in all their glory. It was said that even at that time the quality is now a very pronounced fact. She seemed to possess a sort of magnetic influence over the animal kingdom and could and frequently did put her hands through the bars to pet the beasts with perfect safety.

Matilda Enrolls in Art School

In 1874, when Matilda was age 15 (turning 16 in November), her parents enrolled her in the California School of Design in San Francisco. Today this school, which has produced many famous artists, is called the San Francisco Art Institute. On December 28, 1877, the *San Francisco Call* reported that "the Art Association presented awards to the students of the California School of Design with Miss Matilda Lotz winning first prize which was the William Avery, Gold medal for the best oil painting. She studied under Virgil Williams, immediately making great progress."

110

The San Francisco City Directory of 1878 lists Matilda Lotz living in the same building (1025 Lombard) as her brother Paul, who was beginning his career as a photographer. During the school year of 1880, she lived at 4 Highland Terrace. From the Mark Hopkins Institute Review of Art dated, June 1902 "It is, perhaps, unnecessary to announce just exactly how many years ago it was that Miss Lotz had her studio here in San Francisco prior to her departure for Paris. It was in the old Court Building on Montgomery Street, a roof that also housed Miss Nellie Hopps, and Miss Belle Osborn, ... and others known to fame, but it is undeniably a long time ago." During the summer of 1880, the US Census for San Jose shows her living at home with her parents.

While studying at the School of Design, her talents attracted the attention of Dan Cook, a capitalist and gentleman who made his money from mining gold. He and his wife lived on Nob Hill and delighted in supporting artistic interest. From the *San Jose Mercury News*, February 13, 1895, "Mr. Cook questioned Miss Lotz's teacher closely regarding the young lady's capability, her industry and was so well satisfied with the report that he ended by declaring that he would pay her expenses abroad. Furthermore, he instructed Virgil Williams, the President of the San Francisco Art Association that he did not wish his young portage to be restricted to any such sum as $500 a year, but wished to provide her with an income which should enable her to live comfortably, study to the best advantage and to take trips to Italy, Spain or other lands where pictures might be found which she might wish to study." Under the advice of Mr. Williams and a number of local critics, the

111

young artist was sent to Paris where after a year's study, she had two paintings admitted at the Salon.

She probably left for Paris in late summer or fall of 1880. The *San Francisco Bulletin* reported on July 21, 1883 that "Matilda Lotz, formerly of the California Art School of Design, now in Europe has a painting in the Paris Salon representing two dogs, 'Ronflo' and 'Rough,' which is favorably mentioned by the Paris correspondent of the *Baltimore Sun*." In May of 1884 the *Bulletin* reported, "Our gifted townswoman, Matilda Lotz, now in Paris has an animal picture accepted by the Paris salon, entitled 'Friends of the Artist,' a sketch of which appears in the *'Art Amateur'* for June. The lady is surely making wonderful progress in her noble art."

Telling her story in a full page article in the *San Francisco Call*, December 8, 1901, page 13 it stated: "In Paris, Miss Lotz studied for some time in the Julian Academy, later under Emile Van Marcke, but her work, unlike that of Van Mareke, who is renowned as a colorist seems to be influenced more by that of Rosa Bonheur who from the first was to Miss Lotz a faithful friend and a valuable advisor. Up to the day of Miss Bonheur's death these two artists were firm friends and daily associates. Miss Lotz like her friend early decided not to wed, fancying that a divided attention would be a draw back in her chosen and much loved art, so while she always has many friends and is not an old maid in any sense of the word, she is still single. Moreover, in spite of her artistic temperament there has been no rumor of a romance." In the early 1880's after she arrived in Paris, Matilda not only studied with Van

Marcke but also with Felix Barrias. This information was shared in a 1910 correspondence with the California State Library by Matilda.

On December 22, 1885 the *San Jose Mercury News* reported, "A picture by Miss Matilda Lotz, now in the San Francisco Ladies Art Exhibition and entitled, *Le Premier Dejuner* is pronounced by critics as above criticism, and by far the best picture in the exhibition. Miss Lotz is the sister of Deputy County Treasurer, J. A. Lotz and is in Paris. As an animal painter she is rapidly taking rank with Rosa Bonheur." From an article written in the early 1900's about famous women painters of California, "Born in Tennessee, her family moved to San Jose in 1869. Matilda Lotz began painting early and was tutored by her brother Paul, also an accomplished artist. At the School of Design, she graduated with the highest honors. Then at the Paris Academy of Painting, Lotz became the first woman in the history of the academy to receive two gold medals. She was also an excellent portraitist and landed commissions in Europe among the royalty. In the 1880's in San Francisco, she painted the famous people of California."

Matilda Returns to California

Matilda appears to have made one trip to her beloved San Francisco from Europe. She returned in October or November of 1886. By January 3, 1887, she occupied a studio at 728 Montgomery St. She was living at the same address as her brother Paul, 209 Hyde. Under the personals, in the *San Francisco Bulletin* on October 8, 1886 they wrote, "Matilda Lotz will arrive in a few days from Paris, where she has been studying for several years. It is believed that she comes here to remain permanently." That must have been wishful hoping on someone's part, because it never happened. On November 9, 1886 the *San Francisco Mercury News* stated, "Miss Lotz has come back to her early home and the scene of her earlier work as an artist, with a reputation in her particular line not surpassed by any female artist in this country."

Matilda remained in the country for one year and ten months. During that time she appears to have stayed very busy. Besides her studio in San Francisco she traveled to Forest Grove, Oregon in 1887 to paint the famous burro, Johnny Kellog. It is said that he discovered one of the richest mines in Idaho. This was certified by an Idaho district judge who ruled that Johnny was the discoverer of the famed Bunker Hill and Sullivan property. Also during 1887, she was commissioned by Mrs. George (Phoebe) Hearst to paint a picture of her dogs. The painting was entitled *Two Russian Hounds*. In March of 1898, Mrs. Hearst donated the painting to the San Francisco Art Institute.

In October of 1887, Matilda arrived in New York City where it appears she was one of the Gotham City Art students. On May 13, 1888, the *New York Herald* ran an article, "That energetic and progressive institution, the Goham Art Students made yesterday afternoon and evening its annual exhibit. It was remarkably interesting and strong. ....Matilda Lotz excellent and individual studies of horses, sheep and rabbits...." It appears that Matilda lived and studied in New York City for about ten months. She sailed from New York City to her beloved Paris on August 2, 1888.

An interesting statement from the *Macon* (GA) *Telegraph* dated October 21, 1906, and from the article entitled, "Is the American Woman Overrated? After All, How Much Has She Achieved in Comparison With Others. .....There is only one American woman who holds a place in the front rank of artists, except in the line of portraits, and that one woman is Matilda Lotz, painter of camels and dromedaries in Egypt. But Matilda Lotz was starved out when, some years ago, she attempted to establish her studio in America and is forced to live in Europe, where she is appreciated." This may explain why we only find one recorded time she came back to her home in San Francisco.

A Word from Matilda

The following is one of the few opportunities we have to hear from the artist herself. From the *San Jose Mercury News*, May 20, 1889, an article entitled, "San Jose Girl, Ranks Among the Famous Painters of the Old World" The letter, probably received by her brother or sister who were living in the San Francisco area states, "I have now taken a studio and rooms at Ecouen, a pretty little village near Paris. The country round about is pretty for backgrounds, and as the village is built on a hill the views are very fine. Nearby is a handsome castle. I am sorry to say I could not finish my picture for this year's Salon. I started a canvas of four oxen and spent considerable time upon it. Unfortunately for me, the farmer could not spare his oxen longer, just at the time when I most needed them to finish my picture. It was too late to start another. I felt badly, for my friends will expect to see some of my works at the exposition."

It goes on with a headline, *Working in the Rain*, "It is difficult to paint animals that farmers use for their work. One loses so much time with them, and ought to own the animals to be able to study them well. I have been making studies of plowed ground for my picture. There is nothing more difficult to paint, as the light and even color changes every few minutes. The sky effects here are beautiful, and at this season dark stormy clouds fill the sky. Sometimes I get benefit of them and come home like a drowned rat; in fact I have to work in the rain half the time, I look forward with a great deal of pleasure to the exposition, for I expect to see many fine pictures and to meet many Americans."

Her second trip to the United States appears on December 16, 1889, in the ship manifest for the Umbria, sailing from Liverpool, England. It lists Matilda Lotz landing in New York City. To this date no other record indicates her travel intentions. An article appeared in the *San Jose Evening News* on June 21, 1910, stating, "Miss Lotz, who is now making San Francisco her home is well known to San Joseans having been raised in this city...." This

116

article plus another article from the *San Francisco Chronicle* dated June 19, 1910, was announcing, "A remarkable collection of Matilda Lotz's paintings is being placed on Exhibit at the Memorial Museum at Golden Gate Park." No other record has been found proving that she lived or stayed in San Francisco during this time period.

In 1895, back home in San Jose, it was reported, "At Tangier (Morocco) last year Miss Lotz did some remarkable work and attracted the attention of a Hungarian nobleman who is one of the world's great patrons of the arts. She went to the castle in Hungary to fill some orders and there her work attracted the attention of the 6th Duke of Portland and Duchess. At the invitation of these distinguished connoisseurs of art Miss Lotz has been spending some months at Welbeck Castle, (Nottingham) England, where she has painted to order for the Duke pictures of some of the most famous horses in England—those in his own stables." The report goes on to say, "Evidently Miss Lotz deems Egypt more alluring than even England, for she hurried away to Cairo again as soon as the Duke of Portland's horses were finished. She writes from the south that she is 'painting for dear life' under sunny skies, but that it takes courage to work in the dirty streets of Cairo, where the conditions are anything but pleasant and the flies swarm over the subjects till she hires an Arab to beat them off so that she can get at least an occasional glimpse of the natural lines."

Matilda Meets Future Husband

In 1893-94 Matilda painted in Tangier, Morocco. By October of 1894, she was living in Tata outside Budapest, Hungary at the invitation of Earl Miklos Esterhazy. While she was in Tata she met Ferenc Blaskovits, whom she would later marry. She spent 1895 painting in and around Cairo, Egypt.

In October of 1897, Matilda was reported painting in Tata, Hungary. In 1898, she was in Egypt once again, and in 1901, painting in Africa.

Again from the *San Francisco Call*, December 1901, "The pictures from Miss Lotz's are all painted in a low tone the very highest quality being perhaps their absolute truth in nature. Of the two principal departments of art comprehended in the idealistic and the naturalistic schools Miss Lotz belongs decidedly to the latter. Nature seems to be her inspiration; she loves the field, the mountain, the wood she loves animal life, her horses, dogs and oxen are her personal friends and to their ears are confided her joys and troubles, all her hopes and disappointments.

Miss Lotz paints like a man; there is a strength and vigor, broadness in her work that in some instances equals in the particular style that of Bonheur, who always worked out the detail with a little more finish to get the same effect.

This artist in her sketching tours through Europe has made many friends and has from time to time been presented with some valuable animals. As she likes to keep them all, and now in Paris, besides a studio, has almost a complete menagerie.

Last year Miss Lotz, finding herself in failing in health, decided to take rest and recreation in a trip up the Nile, where she made studies of the camels and also painted some in landscape and architecture although in this line, her work does not compare with her animal pictures. During her travels she stopped for a time in Budapest, where the Count Esterhazy, the head of the government, the ruler next in power to the Emperor Francis Joseph, admired her work so much that he ordered the erection of a studio for her especial benefit. The studio is now locked up, awaiting her return to that country.

Emperor Francis Joseph gave her several commissions and now has a number of Miss Lotz' pictures. Mrs. Phebe Hearst, who for many years has been among the first to recognize talent among our American girls, has always been much interested in the progress of this artist. (Mrs. Hearst was the mother of William Randolph Hearst.) Two canvases, one a Jersey calf, another of hunting dogs, which now hang in the Mark Hopkins Institute of Art were presented to the gallery by Mrs. Hearst. (The Mark Hopkins Institute of Art on Knob Hill was destroyed in the San Francisco earthquake and fire, April 18, 1906. If Matilda's painting remained in the building they may have been destroyed.)

Although Miss Lotz has been sixteen years (1885-1901) absent from her native land it is said that she is still as patriotic as ever. Some San Francisco friends who spent last year abroad remarked upon her observance of the good old American Independence Day. In whatever part of Europe she may be, when the Fourth of July comes around her studio is always gaily decorated in Uncle Sam's colors."

Luckily, the late Dr. Rosalie Carter of Franklin, TN became interested in the Albert Lotz family as she began researching Tod Carter in the late 1960s. It was Dr. Carter's contact with the descendants in California that helped add to the research for this important family. The following two letters were written by Matilda Lotz, which provides insight into her life and art. Matilda responded to a letter from J.L. Gillis who was the State Librarian for the California State Library. He was requesting photos of her work and information concerning her artistic success across the years.

Letter 1:

9 Rue Campagne Premiere
Paris (14 mi)
Mr. J. L. Gillis, State Librarian [California]
Dear Sir,

When I filled out the cards I was interrupted and made a mistake by writing my professors, names in the wrong place and lacking space I fear that I did not write them very definite. So I write these lines to correct them.

I began studying art in the Art School in San Francisco under Mr. Virgil Williams and then came to Paris where I became a pupil of Messrs. Van Marcke and Felix Barrias. I also forgot to mention that one of my pictures 'Oxen at Rest' is in the museum in Golden Gate Park, San Francisco, Cal.

Last week I returned the cards filled out and sent a photograph of myself.

Very Truly yours,

Matilda Lotz
February 15, 1910

Letter 2:

9 Rue Campagne Premiere
Paris (14 mi)
Mr. James Gilly, (Gillis) State Librarian, Sacramento, CA
Dear Sir,

Some time ago when I sent my biography and a photograph of myself to you for the California State Library, you expressed the wish to procure some photographs of some of my pictures, but I regretted not to have any to send at that time.

Recently I had a letter from my niece saying that she had several photographs of some of my pictures, which were made in my brother's gallery before the San Francisco fire, which she offers to send to you. I wrote to her to send the photographs to you so that you can select those which will be most suitable. In case if there are any which cannot be of use, will you please kindly return them to my niece. Her address is Miss Lillian Ahlers 1985 Oak Street San Francisco.

Hoping that you will receive the photographs all right.

Yours Truly

Matilda Lotz
Paris
April 14, 1911

In the information that was sent to Mr. Gillis, Matilda lists what she considered her principal works (1880-1910) that had been exhibited. The following list was written in her own hand.

An Early Breakfast – Salon, Paris

The Artists Friends – Salon, Paris

Deer Hounds – Salon, Paris

Cattle & Sheep – Paris

StableInterior Calves — Budapest, Hungary

A Cozy Corner — Vienna, Austria

Camels at Rest (Painted in Egypt) - Royal Academy, London, England

St. Simon - Welbeck Abbey, Nottingham, England

Donovan — Welbeck Abbey, Nottingham, England

Hounds Morning for their Master, Hungary

Group of Hounds — England

Sick Donkey - Hungary

Oxen at Rest — San Francisco, Calif.

Older years – A Mix of Happiness and Sadness

The latter years of Matilda's life were a mix of some happiness but so much sadness. From *The Evening News*, San Jose, CA, August 2, 1917 we get a glimpse of her last years. "The last time she came home to visit San Francisco and San Jose (1886) she brought with her a splendid Newfoundland dog named Jumbo. In the Joseph Lotz home hangs a portrait of Jumbo. With him is a

123

spaniel. Miss Lotz gave Jumbo to Mrs. Joseph Lotz. She sold the painting to William Randolph Hearst for six hundred dollars. Jumbo is long since dead, but as long as Matilda Lotz's canvas survives, Jumbo will live radiating goodness and truth. Mrs. Frank Lewis of Capitola has one of Matilda Lotz's pictures of dogs. In the Golden Gate Park Museum are several of Matilda Lotz's best paintings, but it is to be hoped that these early pictures will always be kept in San Jose.

During the past few years, she has done little work because of ill health. About four years ago (1913) Miss Lotz married Count Francis Vlasshovitz, painter from Hungary. In fact, he was a very well known Algerian born painter whose name was Ferenc Blaskovits. One of Matilda's paintings, which today hangs in California, was signed Matilda Lotz Birkra. One would suspect that she chose to Americanize and shorten his name. Until the war came, he was the younger son of a noble family. Several of his brothers were killed in the war and Ferenc became the head of this house.

Matilda and Ferenc first met in Tata, Hungary, 1894, where they were both painting professionally. They reconnected in Paris in 1913 and within a short time were married. He was 54 and she was 55 years of age. We know it was Matilda's first marriage. No record has been found of a former marriage for Ferenc. Matilda lived in the heart of Paris, in the artistic district at Campagne Premiere No. 9. By the summer of 1914, everything would change. From the beginning of World War I, Matilda's world would be turned upside down.

The Heartbreak of World War I

Matilda's husband Ferenc Blaskovits was a citizen of Austria. Austria, being an ally of Germany, put the couple in direct conflict with France. During the summer of 1914, Germany invaded France. It appears Ferenc and Matilda decided to move to what they thought was a safe shelter in Algeria. But Algeria was ruled by France and it appeared to the French that Matilda's husband was an enemy of the state. There they were placed under house arrest. On November 17, 1914, Matilda signed a document in Algiers stating she had received her share of the distribution from her brother, Paul's estate.

Sometime in 1915, the couple was exchanged by the French for some other prisoners and allowed to travel to Hungary. One stipulation was that they would have to leave all their personal possessions behind. For Matilda this was a heart breaker, as all her beloved paintings were left in Algeria. From the August 2, 1917, *San Jose Evening News*, "At present they (the couple) are at Budapest, (Tata) but the relatives in San Jose have had no news from them in more than a year." With the United States involved in the War, this must have been a very difficult time knowing their sister was living in the middle of so much conflict.

From the death records and an obituary from Tata, Hungary, (which is outside Budapest) it confirms that Matilda died, February 21, 1923. Her resting place was not listed. She would have been sixty five years of age. The record indicates she died of old age. But from the account of her life in the obit, dated February 24, 1923, we read a sad ending to what had been an adventure filled life. "In the last times the artist suffered from diseases, she only wished to be able to return to Alger. At the time of their escape, her valuable paintings and her belongings had been left there, and she did not get any news from them. The uncertainty drove her to despair, and the constant state of depression tried her weak constitution and after several weeks' illness, she died on Wednesday. Her death deeply affected her friends and admirers. She was a highly educated, world travelled lady whose company was a pleasure for everyone. Her husband, Ferenc Blaskovits is in mourning for her."

It appears that the couple was a great comfort for each other during their ten years together. From her state death record it indicates her religion as Reformed (Calvinist).

Her husband Ferenc died in Tata on June 24, 1931. His cause of death was due to a stroke. From his death record we learn he was Roman Catholic and was 71 years of age at his time of death. His parents' names were Andras Blaskovits and Karolin Bohm. It is interesting to note that on April 13, 1924, a year after Matilda's death, Ferenc wrote a will leaving everything to his niece, Lillian Ahlers who lived in San Francisco. In fact, Lillian was Matilda's niece. She was the daughter of Amelia Lotz Ahlers, sister of Matilda. The estate came to $1,200. One wonders if this was the grieving husband's attempt to help ease the pain he must have felt for the loss of his wife and all of her paintings she so dearly loved.

Matilda was considered a very important artist during her lifetime. She was well respected in Paris, across Europe and in the California art community. It is interesting to note that she was without question, her own person. In her early years, Matilda was a rugged individual who was willing to break with the norms of her time. She seemed to be loved and admired by her family and those who knew her. No doubt her childhood days in Franklin, TN, the epic Battle of Franklin and the killing of her pet calf, had a lasting impact on Matilda as well as the rest of the Lotz family.

Augustus Lotz

Augustus, youngest child of Albert and Margaret Grass (Grasz) Lotz, was born just three years before the epic Battle of Franklin. Unfortunately, their home was located at the center of one of the bloodiest battles in the Civil War. But fortunately for Augustus, he lived in a very caring, protective and creative environment. From the outset Augustus had a special talent for construction and anything mechanical. For everyone who knew the Lotz family, it was apparent Augustus was following in his father's footsteps. From an article later in life, he was described as a child who did not distinguish himself in school because he always wanted to play with machinery. The story goes that Augustus derived his name from his birth date, which happened to be August 15, 1861. Into young adulthood he was always called August.

The Lotz family continued to live in Franklin, TN until late 1869, when it was decided that for their own safety and the lack of financial stability in the area they would get a new start in California. Augustus' father Albert was fearful of the Klan, who saw him as someone who was sympathetic to the Union. In all probability, he was trying to be neutral and was hopeful for a united country. When Augustus was eight years old, Albert packed up his family, sold the home he had built and moved to San Jose, CA.

It is assumed that Augustus helped his dad in the woodshop; building carriages and watching his father construct pianos. Joseph, his stepbrother, joined them in San Jose, February of 1871. During Augustus' formative years his family found it difficult to keep him at his lessons in the Santa Clara Street School, later known as Horace Mann. From an article in *San Jose Evening News* dated August 3, 1917, entitled "When San Jose Was Young, No. 240, San Jose's Great Inventor," we read; "To Augustus Lotz machinery was what art was to his sister, Matilda. So great was his aptitude that he became a full-fledged machinist without even having been an apprentice."

Augustus Opens First Business

At age 18, Augustus was still at home and listed as a machinist in the 1880 U.S. Census. Sometime during the early 1880s he moved to nearby Alameda and set up his first business. By the late 1880s, he was in San Francisco, as was his sister Amelia and brother Paul. In the 1889 San Francisco City Directory he was listed living at 909 Army as a mechanical engineer. By 1891, he was still living at 909 Army and was listed as a machinist. But in 1893, the directory carried a larger ad which listed his business as Augustus Lotz, manufacturer, laundry and electrical machinery, canning machinery and specialty at 211 Main. Then, in the City Directory for 1894, we find Augustus Lotz listed as vice president and manager of Novelty Machine Works, 117-119 Main. Two years later in 1896, listed as machinist, he was still living at 909 Army. By the next year, Augustus was listed as a machinist at the F. A. Robbins Press Works, living at 3813 Army.

On April 26, 1888, he married Margaret Anna Wurm in San Jose. Her parents were Johann (John) G. Wurm, born in Germany, and Jeannette Catherwood Ritchie, born in Scotland. In the 1900 census Augustus and Margaret are listed living at their Army Street address with two children, Hazel E. (Elizabeth), age 8, and Margaret Gladys, age 3. Hazel was born on January 28, 1891, and her sister Gladys was born March 22, 1897, both in San Francisco. Their first child, Clarence, was born on July 28, 1889, and died March

19, 1890, probably in San Francisco. In 1901, August was listed for the first time in the city directory by the name Augustus Lotz, still working for the F.A. Robbins Press Works, but now as foreman. It is interesting to note from this point forward in all printed matter he went by the formal name, Augustus. They were now living across the street at 3814 Army. While living in San Francisco he was elected Master Mason in Oriental Lodge 144.

Augustus First Patent

Beginning in 1901, Augustus was awarded his first US Patent, #676,073 for a Fish-Cleaning Apparatus. He and a man named Wm. Munn were the assignors (appointed to the task of inventing) for the Alaska Pakers Association. In the August 3, 1917, *San Jose Evening News* article entitled, "San Jose's Great Inventor," we read "While there (San Francisco) he invented a machine for cleaning salmon. Into one end passed the fish. It shot like a flash through the machine, which cut off its head, scaled it, split it open and washed it. For this invention Lotz received nothing. The company claimed it because he was working for them."

By 1902, Augustus was working for the American Can Co. and was living with his family at 210 Fair Oaks in San Francisco. Between 1903 and 1908 the U.S. Patent Office approved six of Augustus inventions which were designed to improve the manufacturing companies' operation. Because of the significance of these inventions, we list them in date order with their patent number.

July 21, 1903	Can-Body-Blank-Feed Mechanism #733,983
November 1, 1904	Can Fusing Machine #778,800
November 8, 1904	Can-End-Soldering Machine #774,483
February 20, 1906	Automatic Square-Can Heading and Crimping Machine #812,857
20 Feb 1906	Automatic Round-Can Heading and Crimping Machine #812,858
22 Dec 1908	Can Heading Machine #907259

By the time this patent was approved, Augustus and his family were living in Philadelphia, PA.

Also beginning in 1902, he applied for his first carpet cleaning devise patent. Record shows that he received patent #695,162 on March 11, 1902, an invention that was entitled, "Apparatus for Cleaning Carpets" - with half the credit going to Augustus Lotz and the other half going to Joseph Haas and Julius Kahn all of San Francisco. Augustus would spend the rest of his life designing, improving and manufacturing vacuum dust removal machines. In the 1904 City Directory he was listed as President of the Sanitary Air and Suction Dust Removing Co. Augustus and his family then lived at 2424 Gough. It appears that he was beginning his own vacuum cleaning manufacturing company while still doing work for The American Can Co.

Augustus continued to be a very busy man who probably was making money with his inventions, so he could build up his own new business. On March 8, 1904, he received U.S. Patent #754,325 for his invention entitled, "Wire-Solder-Rolling Machine." This work was done for the Pacific Metal Works of San Francisco. Before all was said and done, Augustus would register a total of eighteen inventions with the U.S. Patent Office.

Then, on May 10, 1904, approval came with Patent #759,452 for a "Pneumatic Carpet-Renovator." This invention was created for his company which was now called, Sanitary Compressed Air and Suction Dust Removing Co. The following is the first few sentences of his patent application, in his own words: "My invention relates to an apparatus which is designed for the removal of dust and refuse from carpets and like permanently-laid or fixed articles. The object of my invention is to remove the dust from such fixed fabrics without loosening or taking them from the floor or other places where they may be fixed. It consists of a centrally-located nozzle in the form of a long narrow slit through which a blast of air or equivalent fluid medium is forcibly directed against the article to be cleansed, whereby the dust is thoroughly loosened and raised from the surface or nap, and in the combination with said blast-nozzle of similar elongated suction-nozzles located upon each side of the blast-nozzle whereby the dust when loosened is instantly drawn into the suction-nozzles and prevented from being spread about or again deposited upon the cleansed article." I believe we can conclude from his creative inventions that Augustus was on the cutting edge of a new carpet cleaning devise, which we call today, the vacuum cleaner.

The following is a complete list of the dust removing devices invented by Augustus Lotz with Patent approval dates.

- March 11, 1902   Apparatus for Cleaning Carpets #695,162

- November 3, 1903   Pneumatic Device for Cleaning Carpets, floors or the like   #742,880 For the Sanitary Compressed Air and Suction Dust Removing Co.

- May 10, 1904   Pneumatic Carpet-Renovator #759,452   Sanitary Compressed Air and Suction Dust Removing Co.

- September 6, 1904   Means for Observing Dust-Laden Air Currents #769,618

- February 26, 1907   Apparatus for Cleaning Dust-Laden Air #845,364   This was for the Sanitary Device Manufacturing Company.

- February 26, 1907   Process of Separating Solid Material Held in Suspension by Air Currents #845,563   Also for the Sanitary Device Manufacturing Company

- February 26, 1907 Apparatus for Separating Dust from Dust-Laden Air Currents #845,562 For the Sanitary Devices Manufacturing Co. of CA.

- December 29, 1908 Valve #908,413 For the Sanitary Devices Manufacturing Co.

- May 3, 1910 Pneumatic Cleaner #956,535 Augustus first filed this patent in Feb 1906.

- February 16, 1915 Governor for Vacuum Cleaning Systems. He first filed this invention in 1907, while still in San Francisco, CA. This was filed with fellow assignor, C. W. Bailey of Philadelphia. Assignors by Mesne Assignments to the Vacuum Cleaner Co. of NY City.

It appears that Augustus Lotz's first company was called Sanitary Compressed Air and Suction Dust Removing Co. Family stories relate that he lost his manufacturing company in the April 18, 1906 San Francisco Earthquake. Then, it appears he rebuilt under the new name Sanitary Devices Manufacturing Company of CA. Family lore indicates that he installed the first central vacuum system in the area. His central vacuum system was installed in the historic Claremont Hotel in Berkeley, CA and several other local businesses.

In April 9, 1905, an article appeared in the *San Jose Mercury News* promoting a new sanitary cleaning wagon. The article establishes a working relationship between Augustus and his brother Joseph. "The San Jose Sanitary

Cleaning Company is a concern which established an office in July 1904. This company cleans houses and carpets by a compressed air and vacuum system. Every particle of dirt and dust is removed..... The officers of the company guaranteed every contract that is undertaken and will furnish estimates of cost at anytime. C G. Sharon is president and manager and Jos. A. Lotz secretary and treasurer....The system was invented by Augustus Lotz and his expectations have been more than realized and nearly every hotel and rooming-house keeper and many housewives are eager to have their rooms and homes cleaned." Along with the article was a photo of a large cleaning wagon, probably as much as seven feet tall and 12 feet long. It appears the wagon was designed to be pulled by horses or a motorized vehicle.

Family Moves to Philadelphia

We find Augustus and his family listed in the Philadelphia, PA City Directory, dated 1908. He is listed as manager of the Sanitary Devices Mfg. Co. The family lived at 3147 Broad. In 1909, they were living at 3503 Disston in Tacony, a community near Philadelphia. The 1910 U.S. Census shows they had moved to 7014 Hegerman, in Tacony. Augustus is listed as a machinery manufacturer. He was 49 years of age and been married to Margaret for 21 years. Margaret was 46, and daughters

Hazel, age 19 and Margaret Gladys age 13. In 1912, they were still living in the same home and Augustus was listed as a mechanical engineer. By 1916 and 1917, they had moved to 4525 Old York Rd. in Philadelphia, with Augustus listed as an engineer.

From the August 3, 1917 *San Jose Evening News* we read, "From San Francisco, Augustus Lotz went to Philadelphia, where he interested himself in a vacuum cleaner which had just been put on the market. The cleaner was a failure, but Mr. Lotz improved it till he made of it a success. Now he is a wealthy man because of the huge royalties accruing to him from the vacuum cleaner."

Augustus died April 26, 1918, in Philadelphia at age 56. Following his death, his ashes were consigned to the Delaware River on April 29, 1918. From the *Philadelphia Inquirer*: "Augustus, husband of Margaret A. Lotz. Relatives and friends, (Masonic) Oriental Lodge. No. 144 F and AM and Tacony Lodge No. 600 F and AM are invited to the funeral, Interment private." Augustus was the only one of the Lotz children to come back and visit Franklin. He and his wife visited the Carter family while they were living in PA.

Margaret removed to San Francisco to live out her years. In 1920, she was living with her sister Elizabeth Wurm Tucker at 4128 23rd St. In the household were Elizabeth's sons, Robert and Fred. Also living in the home were Margaret's and Augustus daughter, Hazel and her family, husband George and children Samuel, George and Janette. In the 1930 Federal Census, Margaret and daughter

Gladys were living together at 1401 10th Ave., San Francisco. Margaret died on November 18, 1943. She is buried in the Woodlawn Memorial Park in Colma, CA (Sec.-J, Row 8B, Grave 35.)

VII ○ Today

Today the Lotz House remains privately owned. The Lotz House Foundation is a 501 (c) 3 nonprofit foundation overseen by a dedicated board of directors. As Lotz sold everything, or gave it away to escape being done in by the KKK, just two pieces of his original furniture are displayed in the house. The first piece is a sofa we have been able to acquire that he carved post-war. Carved of beautiful walnut, it sits proudly in the front hall for all of our visitors to see. And the second piece is a very recent addition. Early in 2011, we were thrilled to learn that for the first time since we've been opened, some living descendants, the great-great granddaughter of Johann Albert Lotz, Nora Bourke King and her husband Steve from Martinez, California were driving cross country to see us. We were thrilled! And when they pulled up in the front yard, I understood why this fabulous couple had decided to drive cross country all the way from California to Tennessee.

Out of the back of their white truck, they pulled out a beautiful black walnut center table. What a table. It was carved in Franklin by the Lotz before the war, survived the battle inside the house, and when Lotz fled Franklin, about to be done in by the Klan, it was the only piece of furniture Lotz took with him to California. And when you look at the table, you can clearly see why. It has a beautiful crotch grained black walnut top, intricately carved C and S scrolled legs, stylized Dolphin head feet and an incrediblehand carved Grecian Urn on the bottom. Every piece of the table is carved. He left no piece of the table untouched. Without question, it is an example of the best woodworking he was capable of producing; his pride and joy. And when you consider he took it with him in the covered wagon across Indian territory in 1869-1870, only to return to Franklin in the back of white truck.

We are thrilled beyond measure to have it back in the home. And we are so very grateful to Nora and Steve for their gracious and generous gift.

Since opening, we were also able to acquire four original Matilda Lotz paintings. All of them are very special in their on rite, but my favorite is "The Wolf" painted by Matilda when she was just 11 years old. It's her earliest known painting to exist and I want to thank Nora, Matilda's great-great niece, who kindly donated the painting to the foundation in 2010. Other Matilda paintings in the collection include "Sheep at Rest," painted my Matilda in California when she is 15 or 16 years of age, and "The Donkey," painted by Matilda in 1880 when she was 22 years old. A wonderful, gracious couple from Carmel California was searching the internet one day and came across the Lotz House website. "The Donkey" had been a part of their collection for many years, but after researching the Lotz House Foundation, they were so moved by our efforts in restoring the home, they wanted to help us. In making their donation, they stressed they wanted to remain anonymous. They graciously sent this piece for the one year anniversary of being open. I cannot thank you enough for your kindness.

The last original piece we have acquired, as of this writing, is a wonderful piece painted by Matilda in Paris. It is a large painting with a lone bull and several cows in background. It's an exciting piece that fortunately remains in its original Parisian gold gilt frame.

But there's so much more in the Lotz House. Today, the Thompson collection proudly resides in the Lotz House. It's a collection that they began in their teens and has been lovingly, carefully and thoughtfully added to for more than 56 years.

Today, visitors to the Lotz House see and learn about the life and times of 19th century through the antiques and decorative arts of the period. Wendell Garrett is a staple on the Antique Road Show. He's also the editor at large at *The Magazine Antiques*. Based out of New York City, the magazine is the foremost publication of antiques. Regrettably Mr. Garrett has yet to visit us at the Lotz House, but he has personally followed the collection for 30 years and has seen it in other homes across the country. According to Garrett, "it's the finest collection of American made 19th century antiques in privately owned hands in the country." That's an endorsement for which we are most proud.

The collection includes many pieces of John Henry Belter furniture, a huge assortment of old Paris Porcelain, exquisite English and American Silver, an extraordinarily rare example of birds mounted by the famous John James Audubon and a large number of Franklin battlefield relics and items that were picked up off the battlefield after the fact.

Speaking of Battlefields, it would remiss of me not to mention Thomas Y. Cartwright. You've seen him on the History Channel, Discovery and A&E speaking about the Civil War and the Battle of Franklin. Thomas is one of the preeminent historians on the Battle of Franklin, and he's forgotten more about it than most people will ever know. I am so pleased and honored to tell you that Thomas is now working with us at the Lotz House doing walking battlefield tours of Franklin. Almost everyone that takes Thomas' tour comes back to the Lotz House and says it's about as close as they can imagine to walking on the battlefield with the soldiers themselves. If you have never taken one of Thomas' tours, you don't know what you've missed. Stop by and take one, you'll be glad you did!

VIII ○ The Future

As of this writing, the Lotz House has been opened for 36 months. And I am happy to let you know that the numbers of visitors we have continues to grow each month. We are staffed by a group of friendly and knowledgeable volunteers that give our guests a wonderful, riveting tour of the battle, the Lotz family, Matilda and the Collection.

According to Trip Advisor (www.tripadvisor.com), we are one of the top attractions in all of Middle Tennessee. Our long term plans calls for refurbishing the ceilings in the home, installing appropriate lighting in all of the rooms, wall papering the rooms that currently don't have paper hanging, and at some point, we want to remove the paint from all of Mr. Lotz original woodwork. We'd also like to erect a split rail fence around part of the property, the way Mr. Lotz did in 1855.

Acquiring more of Matilda's art and paintings also is a top priority. They are few and far between. As monies become available, we hope to add more to the collection.

We have been richly rewarded by an ever growing number of Lotz House Foundation members. We want to continue to grow that number. We want and need the people of Franklin, Williamson County, Tennessee and folks from across the country to embrace our mission. Thinking big and looking a long way down the road, it would be wonderful to acquire more of the original five acres that Mr. Lotz purchased from Mr. Carter. Bob, Thomas and I are determined to continue our quest to research the Lotz and their moving and inspirational story. In closing you must know this. It's our goal that the Lotz House and the collection will always and forever remain in tact.

Appendix

Chronology of the Lotz House Ownership
Franklin, Tennessee

1858 - F.B. Carter sold 5-acre lot to Albert Lotz

1870 - Albert Lotz sold house and lot to Robert G. Buchanan

1899 - Robert G. Buchanan sold house and lot to Thomas J. Carothers

1915 - J.C. Carothers gave trust deed to P.E. Cox, Trustee to property

1920 - P.E. Cox Trustee to National Bank of Franklin

1925 - National Bank of Franklin to E.E. Green and Thomas B. Johnson

1931 - T.B. Johnson estate to D.T. Crockett

1945 - D.T. Crockett to Howard Hill

1946 - Howard Hill to J.A. McGee

1952 - Bridgett McGee to Virginia Freeman

1961 - Virginia Freeman to Sam Livingston and Morris Levine

1972 - Livingston & Levine to Glen Noble and Roy Barker

1974 - Glen Noble to Roy Barker

1974 - Roy Barker to The Heritage Foundation

1975 - Heritage Foundation to Larry Brown

1982 - Larry Brown to Wayne Glasgow, Jr.

1988 - Wayne Glasgow, Jr. to Lotz Corner Properties L.T.D. (Dan Clark)

1991 - Dan Clark to J.T. Thompson

RECORD OF KNOWN PAINTINGS

by

MATILDA LOTZ

c 1870 – 1910

The following is a list of the oil paintings produced by Matilda Lotz from about 1870 to 1910. This list is not exhaustive. Surely there will be other paintings found from a lifetime dedicated to capturing on canvas the natural tenderness she felt toward God's creatures. We are blessed to have a 1910, hand written copy by Matilda of her principle works for the California State Library in Sacramento.

Following her marriage in 1913, until her death, there is little known about her work. Much of her personal collection was lost during Ferenc and Matilda's escape from Algeria to Hungary. Our hope is that persons who read this book and know of other paintings or persons who own paintings by Matilda Lotz will be in contact with the Lotz House Museum.

Paintings hanging in the Lotz House Museum

Donkey – Painted in CA, 1880

Sheep at Rest, CA, c1880

Wolf, CA, c1870

The Herd, Paris, 1885,86

Paintings listed by Matilda Lotz as her principle works and their location in 1910

An Early Breakfast, exhibited in the Salon, Paris, France, c1882 (reported to be in a gallery in Washington D.C. in 1973) It is possible this gallery was the Corcoran Art Gallery. This painting has also been called, *"A Dog's Breakfast."* It portrays a group of dogs gathered about a broken box of garbage which has been thrown into the street.

The Artists Friends, exhibited in the Salon, Paris, c1884 (also listed as, *Friends of the Artist),* This painting sold for $500 in May, 1885 at the San Francisco Art Exhibition.

Deer Hounds, exhibited in the Salon, Paris, c1883-'84

Cattle & Sheep, Paris

Stable Interior Calves, Budapest, Hungary, c1894

A Cozy Corner - Hounds, Kinstler House, Vienna, Austria

Camels at Rest, Egypt c1895, Royal Academy, London, England

Donovan, The 6th Duke of Portland's prize horse, 1894, Welbeck Abbey, Notingham, England. (This painting shows a bay horse standing to right in a stable, with the terrier dog, Sting near his fore feet.)

St Simon, The 6th Duke of Portland's horse, 1894, Welbeck Abbey, England.

Hounds Morning for their Master, Hungary

Group of Hounds, England

Sick Donkey, Hungary

Oxen at Rest, San Francisco, CA, Shown at the Spring Exhibition at the Mark Hopkins Institute of Art, March 1902.

Other paintings by Matilda Lotz

Barn Scene (Sheep), 1877, 6 ¾" x 8.5" In 2009 painting owned by Mr. & Mrs. John Scott, San Francisco, CA.

Resting Cow Study, 8" X 12", 1878, San Francisco, CA

A Sheep at Rest, 17" X 21 ¾"

Le Premier Dejuner, shown at the San Francisco Ladies Art Exhibition in December, 1885

"Miss Lotz is working on a painting of dogs for Mrs. George Hearst." Daily Alta, November 6, 1887

Johnny Kellog, Forest Grove, OR, 1887

Two Russian Hounds, donated to the San Francisco Art Institute in March 1886 by Mrs. Phoebe Hearst. Mrs. Hearst also donated a canvas of a Jersey calf to the Art Institute which hung at the Mark Hopkins Art Institute Gallery.

The Pasture shown in San Francisco in October, 1912.

Jumbo, This is a picture of Matilda's Newfoundland dog. In the painting stands a spaniel with Jumbo. The dog was given to Matilda's sister-in-law, Mrs. Joseph Lotz in San Jose. Later Mrs. Lotz sold Jumbo to Mrs. William Randolph Hearst for $600.

Cattle in the Field, 18 ½" X 28 ½", Painted in Paris, sold in New York to Scott Smith who lives in Spring Hill, TN.

Gateway to Alhambra. Painted by Matilda while she was traveling in Spain. This is one of the paintings she had at the Spring Exhibition at the San Francisco Institute of Art in May of 1897.

Matilda Lotz paintings sold at auction

Dog Waiting by the Gate 25.5" x 31.5"

Tending the Camels, 19"x 25"

Sheep, 10.7" x 15.2"

Bishna (The Goat herder), 13.5" x 21.5"

Chinatown Interior, 7.5" x 10"

Deer in the Woods, 13" x 16"

Algerie 19" x 24"

Cows in the Pasture, 10" x 15"

Waiting for Dinner, 18" x 24"

Lancer: Portrait of a Dog, 7.5" x 9"

Friends, 24.5" x 32"

Resting by the Cistern In Tanger, 1893, 109 x 156 cm.

Made in the USA
Charleston, SC
26 November 2011